THE MAGIC OF ROGUES

MAGIC in HISTORY

SOURCEBOOKS SERIES

THE ARRAS WITCH TREATISES
Andrew Colin Gow, Robert B. Desjardins, and François V. Pageau

HAZARDS OF THE DARK ARTS:
ADVICE FOR MEDIEVAL PRINCES ON WITCHCRAFT AND MAGIC
Richard Kieckhefer

ORIGINS OF THE WITCHES' SABBATH
Michael D. Bailey

The Magic in History Sourcebooks series features compilations and translations of key primary texts that illuminate specific aspects of the history of magic and the occult from within. Each title is tightly focused, but the scope of the series is chronologically and geographically broad, ranging from ancient to modern and with a global reach. Selections are in readable and reliable English, annotated where necessary, with brief contextualizing introductions.

SERIES EDITORS
RICHARD KIECKHEFER
Northwestern University
CLAIRE FANGER
Rice University

THE MAGIC OF ROGUES

NECROMANCERS IN EARLY TUDOR ENGLAND

FRANK KLAASSEN AND SHARON HUBBS WRIGHT

The Pennsylvania State University Press

University Park, Pennsylvania

Library of Congress Cataloging-in-Publication Data

Names: Klaassen, Frank F., author. | Wright, Sharon Hubbs, 1963– author.
Title: The magic of rogues : necromancers in early Tudor England / Frank Klaassen and Sharon Hubbs Wright.
Other titles: Magic in history sourcebooks series.
Description: University Park, Pennsylvania : The Pennsylvania State University Press, [2021] | Series: Magic in history sourcebooks series | Includes bibliographical references and index.
Summary: "Examines legal documents and magic texts relevant to two cases where authorities in Tudor England confronted practicing magicians. Explores how magicians thought about the world, where they got their ideas, and how their magic was supposed to work"—Provided by publisher.
Identifiers: LCCN 2020051782 | ISBN 9780271089294 (paperback)
Subjects: LCSH: Magic—England—History—16th century—Sources. | Magicians—Legal status, laws, etc.—England—History—16th century—Sources.
Classification: LCC BF1622.E5 K53 2021 | DDC 133.4/30942—dc23
LC record available at https://lccn.loc.gov/2020051782

Published by The Pennsylvania State University Press,
University Park, PA 16802–1003

The Pennsylvania State University Press is a member of the Association of University Presses.

It is the policy of The Pennsylvania State University Press to use acid-free paper. Publications on uncoated stock satisfy the minimum requirements of American National Standard for Information Sciences—Permanence of Paper for Printed Library Material, ANSI Z39.48–1992.

FOR BARBARA TODD

CONTENTS

ACKNOWLEDGMENTS

We thank the staff at the National Archives of Britain, the British Library, the Bodleian Library, the London Metropolitan Archives, and the Borthwick Institute for their wisdom and patience. The work of Owen Davies and Alec Ryrie has been very valuable in this project. In various ways John Billingsley, Claire Fanger, Richard Kieckhefer, Michael Klaassen, Maud Burnett McInerney, and Shannon McSheffrey have all provided critical assistance, criticism, and advice in this project. Elyse Jensen provided digital sketches of the magic figures. We also thank Dana Henricks (copyeditor) and Jess Klaassen-Wright (indexer).

Our debt to Barbara Todd is even deeper. A mentor to both of us, we dedicate this book to you with gratitude for your wisdom and generous guidance.

This volume was made possible by financial support from the Social Sciences and Humanities Research Council of Canada and Saint Thomas More College.

General Introduction

This volume brings together two different types of records concerning premodern magic that have rarely been considered together in any substantive way: manuscripts of magic and legal proceedings against magicians. The body of evidence for magic practice is extensive, including scores of mostly anonymous manuscripts written in Latin and English in sixteenth-century England. These manuscripts reveal a good deal about the way the magicians thought about the world, where they got their ideas from, and how their magic was supposed to work. But the magicians behind them remain shadowy and largely anonymous. Legal records, by contrast, reveal little about the magic but much more about the lives and circumstances of those involved in magic, how they came to be involved with it, and what others, particularly secular and church authorities, thought about it.

The scholarship on magic has tended to be divided along the same lines. A long-established stream of investigation prompted by interest in the witch trials has focused on the history of magic and its relationship with authority. This developed into explorations of the social aspects of magic practice among lower-level practitioners such as cunning folk and into the broader question of disenchantment. On the other hand, the exploration of learned magic manuscripts has only begun seriously in the past three decades and has concentrated on the intellectual history of magic, its use of prior Arabic and Hebrew sources, how it was transmitted, its relationship to conventional religion or intellectual traditions, its condemnation by the guardians of orthodoxy, or the way the practice of magic has changed over the centuries.

The integrated study of intellectual and legal sources is thus timely and also offers us a more rounded picture of illicit learned magic. It also forefronts the encounters of magicians with authority in a way that separates them from narratives about witchcraft and the witch trials, into which typically (and often unreflectively) they have been collapsed. Those accused of witchcraft were commonly not magic practitioners at all, and their cases present a picture of magic practice that bears little resemblance to real practices. Moreover, understood in the longue durée and over broad geographic areas, the witch trials were relatively unusual, scattered, and sporadic.[1] The magicians considered in this volume were all real magic practitioners in the sense that they had manuscripts of magic, peddled magic services, and set about to practice magic. Their encounters with the law were also more representative of how magic was treated in the centuries prior to the witch trials.

NECROMANCY AND ITS PRACTITIONERS

The magic presented and discussed in this book is typically found in late medieval and early modern necromantic handbooks. Despite the name, necromancy rarely has anything to do with the dead. Instead these collections are largely dedicated to spirit conjuring as well as other assorted practices, such as the creation of magic rings or astrological talismans.[2] This literature falls under the broad category of learned magic, a term that is potentially misleading. As this collection reveals, the practitioners were often low-level clergy or modestly educated laypeople who might be better described as middlebrow and who were part of what Richard Kieckhefer has described as a "clerical underworld."[3] During the course of the sixteenth century, necromantic material was increasingly translated into English, but knowledge of Latin remained almost indispensable.[4] Most of the

1. For a very useful discussion of this question, see H. C. Erik Midelfort, "Witch Craze? Beyond the Legends of Panic," *Magic, Ritual, and Witchcraft* 6 (2011): 11–33.

2. Richard Kieckhefer, *Forbidden Rites: A Necromancer's Manual of the Fifteenth Century* (Stroud: Sutton, 1997); Frank Klaassen, *The Transformations of Magic: Illicit Learned Magic in the Later Middle Ages and Renaissance* (University Park: Pennsylvania State University Press, 2013), 82–155.

3. Richard Kieckhefer, *Magic in the Middle Ages* (Cambridge: Cambridge University Press, 2000), xi. On this group, see also Frank Klaassen, "Learning and Masculinity in Manuscripts of Ritual Magic of the Later Middle Ages and Renaissance," *Sixteenth Century Journal* 38, no. 1 (2007): 49–76.

4. Frank Klaassen, *Making Magic in Elizabethan England* (University Park: Pennsylvania State University Press, 2019), 1–14.

necromantic handbooks continued to be written in Latin. Even if one could find a text written in English, it usually required an ability to recite prayers, psalms, and other liturgical formulae in Latin and ideally from memory. As we shall see in the Mixindale case, ability in magic, or "cunning," was powerfully associated with learning and clerical status, and thus priests and other Latinate or literate people had significant advantages in the magic marketplace. For the same reasons, necromancy was also an almost uniformly male pursuit.[5]

The literature of necromancy arose from the confluence of Arabic and Jewish magic, particularly from Iberia, with magic and religious practices in the Latin West. The resulting written traditions of magic were not always stable or internally consistent but were framed by a basic set of assumptions that, for the most part, reflected conventional medieval Christian thinking. The medieval cosmos was an integrated system in which the moral, physical, and spiritual were inextricably intertwined. God ruled. But his cosmos operated according to a set of preordained natural mechanisms. These included the influence of the heavenly bodies, which influenced life below the circle of the moon in a manner analogous to the weather. In the same sense that heavy rain would tend to drive people to indoor activities, astrological conditions made certain kinds of human behavior or events easier and more likely to take place. These conditions also affected spiritual creatures like angels or demons, which populated the cosmos and which necromantic magic claimed to be able to influence or even control. So, for example, the necromantic handbooks tell us that it is much easier to conjure demons during a waxing moon. Similarly, the universe had a host of hidden interconnections that could be used by the magician. Certain demons were more likely to appear in hours when particular and related planets were reigning and when the way was prepared with the right sort of suffumigation (i.e., something burned like incense) or magical tools. In the same way, the names of spirits or their inscribed characters were ontologically connected to them and could be used to influence or control them.

---

5. For a specific discussion of ritual magic and the clerical environment, see Klaassen, "Learning and Masculinity."

These natural structures were subsumed under the umbrella of Christian ideas, which held that demons could only be truly controlled by Christians invoking the name of Jesus.[6] As a result, it was also necessary for the magician to be in a state of grace (i.e., physical and spiritual purity), achieved through the sacraments, prayer, abstinence, fasting, and godly behavior. In addition, the most powerful rituals were those established by the Church for use in daily worship, known as the liturgy, and someone who knew them was literally more spiritually powerful than other people. A good Christian who had made the right spiritual preparations and then performed the right rituals using the right words and gestures would be able not only to cast out demons, as one might in exorcism, but also to get these powerful creatures to do something wondrous and useful.[7] This, at least, is what the necromantic handbooks argued. These putatively holy rituals contrast starkly with the self-interested goals of this form of magic (e.g., finding and getting treasure, locating stolen goods or thieves, acquiring power or influence, entertainment, and even sexual gratification).

The cases in this volume reveal a good deal about the transmission, exchange, copying, and use of magic books. We know, for example what books or what kinds of books the magicians employed. Their magic was drawn from a variety of sources, some of which are identifiable: the *Treasury of Spirits* (*Thesaurus spirituum*) and *Sworn Book of Honorius* (*Liber iuratus Honorii*) were clearly familiar to them.[8] They employed well-known conjurations of the Four Kings and the spirit Oberion, as well as equipment such as parchment circles also found described in manuscripts. We can also trace the transmission and use of printed books on magic, such as Henry Cornelius Agrippa von

6. Acts 19:11–17; Mark 16:17.

7. Kieckhefer, *Forbidden Rites*; Klaassen, *Transformations of Magic*, 115–55.

8. The *Treasury of Spirits* has yet to be rendered in a scholarly edition but survives in numerous manuscript versions. See, for example, London, Wellcome Library, Welcome 110, which contains the Latin version (fols. 57r–98v) and an English epitome (fols. 1r–35v) both interspersed with other texts. See also London, British Library, Sloane 3853, fols. 3r–45v. For the *Sworn Book of Honorius*, see Gösta Hedegård, ed., *Liber iuratus Honorii—A Critical Edition of the Latin Version of the Sworn Book of Honorius* (Stockholm: Almovist & Wiksell International, 2002). For a brief discussion of the literature of ritual magic circulating in England, see *Transformations of Magic*, 115–27.

Nettesheim's *On Occult Philosophy* (*De occulta philosophia*). Finally, the clerics in the Mixindale case can be seen actually compiling and in some senses *creating* their own magic book by combining rituals in their books with material that they copied from a liturgical volume. All of these will be discussed in more detail in the chapters where they appear.

Despite their illicit status, the scores of necromantic manuscripts that survive from the sixteenth century attest to their popularity. That they were increasingly written in English as the century progressed evinces both a growing popular interest in this literature beyond the confines of the clerical world where they originated and also their introduction into a network of information exchange among laypeople. This picture is fully confirmed by the legal documents, which reveal a lively network of partnerships and exchange of books and information among magicians, both clerical and lay, with a wide range of education.

Undoubtedly, a portion of those who copied manuscripts of necromantic magic did so for private interest or practice, but the group that most commonly came to the attention of the authorities for this were cunning folk, a group that included necromantic practitioners as well as others who seem to have steered entirely clear of necromancy.[9] The term that sixteenth-century people in England most often used to describe skill in magic is "cunning." This derived from the Anglo-Saxon *cunnan*, which meant simply "to know." When the term was applied to magicians, it typically preserved the older sense of learning (i.e., literacy). Unsurprisingly, cunning folk thus tended more often to be men, either clerical or lay, who had more access to education. Working either for pay or other forms of social capital, cunning folk provided a range of services, including identifying or locating thieves, finding lost or stolen property, curing illnesses, and treasure hunting. Cunning folk might also dabble in astrology and love magic. More crucially, they employed a variety of magical techniques that did not involve

9. Our discussion of cunning folk here and throughout this volume derives heavily from Owen Davies, *Cunning-Folk: Popular Magic in English History* (London: Hambledon and London, 2003).

spirit conjuring of any kind and so they cannot be directly equated with necromancers.[10]

In many respects the professional magic practitioners examined in this volume are representative of cunning folk in general: they are men with modest but higher than usual levels of learning; they employ that learning in their magic or to convince their clients of their abilities; people travel many miles to consult with them; and they rely on their reputations to attract business. However, in one crucial respect, the practitioners disclosed in the following documents do not represent the majority of cunning folk. Their activities came to the attention of the authorities, and they were punished for them. Complaints to authorities about cunning folk were relatively rare, probably due to their need to carefully maintain their reputations, and they tended to attract little negative attention from the authorities.[11] It is possible that the attention received by the magic practitioners discussed in this book was simply a matter of bad luck, but evidence suggests that they were also less circumspect and more ambitious than most cunning folk.

MAGIC AND AUTHORITY IN THE EARLY SIXTEENTH CENTURY

Despite necromantic magic's constant reaffirmation of the power of God and the Christian religion, ecclesiastical authorities never regarded it as legitimate, either before or after the Reformation. Midcentury declarations by English bishops called for the gravest penalties possible for magic.[12] Contemporary secular authorities shared the English prelates' desire to root out and prosecute practitioners, at least in principle. This was made manifest in Henry VIII's 1542 legislation, which condemned magic practitioners to death. Public denouncements and legislation, however, are not the same thing as coordinated

10. Ibid., 93–118; Sharon Hubbs Wright and Frank Klaassen, *Everyday Magicians in Tudor England: Legal Records and Magic Manuscripts* (forthcoming).

11. Davies, *Cunning-Folk*, 1–28.

12. *Reformatio Legum Ecclesiasticarum, Ex Authoritate Primum Regis Henrici 8. Inchoata: Deinde Per Regem Edouardum 6. Prouecta, Adauctaque in Hunc Modum, Atque Nunc Ad Pleniorem Ipsarum Reformationem in Lucem Ædita* (London, 1641), 33. Cited in Francis Young, *Magic as a Political Crime in Early Modern England* (London: Taurus, 2018), 79–80.

suppression and extirpation. In reality, comparatively few cases for any form of magic appeared in the church courts and no one was ever prosecuted under Henry's law. This stark divergence between word and deed requires further examination.

In England, prior to 1542, magic was not a crime per se under common law. It fell to the ecclesiastical courts to control and punish magic because in theological terms it was superstitious, idolatrous, and potentially heretical. As the large set of records from the case of the Yorkshire treasure hunters in chapter 3 makes clear, the archbishop and his officials could and did take cases of necromantic magic practice seriously. Nonetheless, even in this case where all the participants were clearly guilty of performing magic, the heaviest penalty that the archiepiscopal court could inflict was major excommunication, which was dissolved by public penance. At the same time, cases such as this one were rare. Despite clear manuscript and legal evidence that magic practice was reasonably common, there does not appear to have been sufficient institutional will to pursue a systematic program of rooting it out. The church's resources were not infinite, but had there been a widespread conviction that such a program was necessary and worth the effort, more concerted efforts could have been made. The laws and mechanisms were certainly in place.[13]

Ecclesiastical energies were directed instead toward less invasive efforts to steer the faithful away from the practice of magic, or the error of believing in it. The late medieval literature written to help parish priests guide their flocks and the devotional and proscriptive literature written for lay readers taught that magic was bad and to be avoided.[14] This literature provided, for example, lurid stories about magicians, their failures, and eventual punishment or redemption. The wide-reaching influence of pastoral and didactic literature meant that most fifteenth- and sixteenth-century people had a reasonably good idea about what they were supposed to avoid and why.

So why was so little real action taken against magic practitioners? One reason was probably that the most common and public forms of

13. Davies, *Cunning-Folk*, 1–66; Young, *Magic as a Political Crime*, 24–26.

14. Catherine Rider, *Magic and Religion in Medieval England* (London: Reaktion, 2012).

magic were not very problematic, and the most problematic forms of magic were less common and more private. The most widespread form of magic in the middle ages was the use of charms, which contained simple verbal formulae usually derived from biblical passages or the liturgy for common ailments or medical emergencies ranging from nosebleeds to childbirth. In general, while it clearly regarded charms as superstitious, the late medieval church was tolerant of such magic, because of its good intents, its affirmation of conventional religion, and the fact that it did not invoke demons or other spirits.[15] More grievous forms of magic were less common and tended to be contracted and performed more or less in private. This was particularly the case with necromantic magic. Everyone knew that this was an illicit practice and that it was prudent to pursue it in careful seclusion. The effect of this situation was that eradicating charms and other similar low-level magic would have been impossible due to their integration into daily life and the sheer volume of potential cases. Detecting and eradicating other more dubious forms of magic was very difficult due to their private nature and the fact that they were less common.

Often, in instances where ecclesiastical officials recorded the use of magic, the issue that brought the case into the court was not magic per se but some other complaint in which magic had played a part.[16] For example, we know of the use of magic for theft identification because the identified "thieves" came to court to seek redress for slander, not because court officials had prosecuted magic practitioners. The extensive surviving literature of magic and anecdotal evidence from the period makes clear that most magic practitioners operated freely and without ever having a confrontation with the authorities. So long as magicians were not socially disruptive, raising concerns about fraud, slander, and in extreme cases heresy, they were generally able to pursue their art without much interference.

The same conditions prevailed in the common law courts, which were even less likely to undertake action against magic, not least because it was not a crime in England until 1542. If the magicians and

15. Catherine Rider, "Medical Magic and the Church in Thirteenth-Century England," *Social History of Medicine* 24, no. 1 (2011): 92–107.

16. For a sampling of common magic before sixteenth-century ecclesiastical courts, see Wright and Klaassen, *Everyday Magicians*.

their clients whose cases we examine in this book had been a little more circumspect, they probably would never have been brought to justice at all. This stands in stark contrast to the spirit of Henry VIII's 1542 Act, a closer examination of which can provide some insight into the concerns of secular authorities in the early Tudor period.

A few aspects of this Act can help make sense of the seeming lack of action taken by the secular courts on magic. First, the motivations behind it remain unknown. While it is commonly referred to as "witchcraft" legislation, no careful reading of it can sustain this description, particularly if the term "witchcraft" is understood to imply that it primarily targeted female practitioners. The principal form of magic it was concerned with was learned magic, particularly necromantic magic, and within that set of practices, treasure hunting. All of the magic it describes, including love magic, reflects the highly male-centered practices that one finds in magic manuscripts.[17] Second, while this law was never actually used against any magicians, the amount of attention it gives to treasure hunters reflects the broader relationship of magic and authority in the period. Prior to the advent of witch trials in the 1560s, treasure-hunting magic appeared more often in legal cases than any other form of magic except the identification of thieves (also mentioned in this Act). Third, while Henry's Act expressed concern with how magic offended God, it gave as much, if not more, attention to the "disquietness of the realm" that magic provoked, the fact that magicians "have digged up and pulled down an infinite number of crosses within this realm," and the "hurt and damage" such actions did to the King's subjects. This is to say, it

---

17. In late medieval European antimagic literature, illicit magic was increasingly *framed* as feminine by key detractors. See Michael D. Bailey, "The Feminization of Magic and the Emerging Idea of the Female Witch in the Late Middle Ages," *Essays in Medieval Studies* 19 (2002): 120–34. However, aside from the use of the term "witchcraft" among numerous other terms for magic, all of the magic mentioned in the 1542 Act, *including love magic*, reflects what one finds in manuscripts of magic written by and for men. See Richard Kieckhefer, "Erotic Magic in Medieval Europe," in *Sex in the Middle Ages: A Book of Essays*, ed. Joyce E. Salisbury (New York: Garland, 1991), 30–55. See also Wright and Klaassen, *Everyday Magicians*. For an argument that the Act reflects feminizing ideas of magic based on its reference to love magic, see P. G. Maxwell-Stuart, *The British Witch: The Biography* (Stroud: Amberley, 2014), 114.

focused heavily on social disruption and damage to property, precisely the issues that most commonly brought magicians into court. In short, the Act itself reflects a way of thinking about magic that emphasized its disruptive social effects and the habit of waiting for the disruption to take place before dealing with it.

Henry's Act suggests that Parliament and the Crown were not only very concerned about magic but also were prepared to punish offenders to the full extent of the law. However, this did not happen; very few magicians and their clients were actually punished for their activities. It may be that the draconian nature of Henry's legislation made the justices disinclined to use it. Execution for a clear case of theft of a significant amount of money was one thing, but the same punishment for attempting to locate stolen goods might well have seemed extreme even in the sixteenth century. In any event, the Act was never employed and was overturned a few years later under Edward VI. England returned to the old circumstances where magic was not a crime in itself.

Curiously, even cases that appear to be clear-cut instances of treason involving magic did not always result in grave punishments in this period. As we shall see, William Neville and the magician Richard Jones eventually walked free despite clearly treasonous offenses only the worst of which were Jones's prediction of Henry VIII's imminent demise and Neville's efforts to find financial and military resources for seizing personal advantage afterward. The same happened with Robert Allen, who was detained for predicting the death of Edward VI, and again with John Prestall in the early years of Elizabeth's reign.[18] The latter, more than any of these magicians, was guilty of magical and treasonous skullduggery and association with seditious Catholic forces. It is possible that secular officials simply continued to regard magic as a matter for the Church courts. It is certainly clear that, despite abortive efforts to change the situation (like Henry's legislation), secular authorities were cautious in bringing to trial cases where someone was accused of using treasonable magic, and even

---

18. On Allen, see Wright and Klaassen, *Everyday Magicians*. On Prestall, see Young, *Magic as a Political Crime*, 91–145; Michael Devine, "John Prestall: A Complex Relationship with the Elizabethan Regime" (MA thesis, Victoria University of Wellington, 2010).

more so in applying the death penalty in such cases. It is also clear that what motivated the initial investigation of William Neville and the later magicians was their potentially treasonous activities rather than magic per se.

Another motivating factor for the arrest of William Neville and his compatriots was clearly prophecy or the spreading of destabilizing rumors. Other cases suggest that prophecy and rumormongering were regarded as greater threats to pubic order than magic. Beginning in 1530, the Privy Council expended considerable energy seeking out, and sometimes brutally punishing, self-styled prophets and those who started rumors of impending political instability, new draconian taxes, or the death of the king. If the numbers of cases, the depth of the institutional paper trails, circular letters to courts from Cromwell, public punishments, and executions for these crimes are any indication, rumor and prophecy were of considerably greater concern to him than magic.[19] Similar to the ecclesiastical courts, which were also concerned with rumor and social discord, cases involving magic most frequently seem to have come to the attention of the secular authorities because they were wound up with other issues. Investigations and trials for magic alone were very rare.

MAGICIANS AND THEIR COMMUNITIES

The cases examined in this book demonstrate that the line between cunning man and learned magician was fuzzy in the sixteenth century. Great intellectual magicians like John Dee and Henry Cornelius Agrippa represented their magic as a kind of mystical religion far above the common, pay-for-service magician. But arguably, they were merely cunning men of a higher order: neither of them entirely disdained to serve as astrologers for the high and mighty. Similarly, among lower-level cunning men, we find magicians who were not only literate but Latinate. In chapter 1, Nash does not represent himself as

19. Sharon L. Jansen, *Political Protest and Prophecy Under Henry VIII* (Woodbridge, UK: Boydell Press, 1991); G. R. Elton, *Policy and Police: The Enforcement of the Reformation in the Age of Thomas Cromwell* (Cambridge: Cambridge University Press, 1972), 46–82.

a learned magician, but Jones certainly does. He has rooms at Oxford, clearly owns magic books, and is familiar with the literature of learned magic, including the work of Agrippa. Jones also evidently practiced alchemy, given the reported presence of stills and alembics in his rooms and his offer to perform alchemy for the crown. In a case we consider below, William Stapleton was a learned monk who ultimately served in various capacities as a treasure hunter and personal magician. In chapter 3, John Wilkinson does not appear to have hired himself out as a cunning man, but John Steward, a former grammar school teacher, certainly did. His knowledge of learned magic was clearly part of what made him attractive as a member of the treasure hunters' fellowship. So, although historians of magic manuscripts have tended to style their scribes as "learned magicians" rather than cunning folk, it is difficult to know where to draw the line. Such people, repeatedly described as "cunning" by their contemporaries, were probably responsible for copying and transmitting many of the surviving manuscripts of learned magic. As we shall see, the case of William Neville in chapter 1 also reveals that the line between magician and peddler of prophecies cannot be clearly delimited.

Examination of the legal documents, particularly those in this volume, also allows us to uncover communities of magicians in action. Five professional magicians and peddlers of prophecies are mentioned in chapter 1, a number of whom knew and communicated with each other. In chapter 3, Wilkinson and Steward each have their own communities of magic practice before joining forces and creating a third one, the Mixindale Fellowship. Wilkinson claims to have been involved in the world of clerical necromancy from his childhood, when he was used as a child scryer and may have had access, through the library of the Austin Friars at York, to one of the largest collections of magic books in England.[20] John Steward also communicated about magic with other laymen. The same sorts of communities appear in the Stapleton case discussed below. All of these magicians were part

---

20. It is possible that Wilkinson got his copy of the *Sworn Book of Honorius* there. K. W. Humphreys, *The Friars' Libraries*, Corpus of British Medieval Library Catalogues (London: British Library in association with the British Academy, 1990), 86–101. On this collection, see also Klaassen, *Transformations of Magic*, 65–77.

of a complex and integrated economy of magic. They exchanged books for copying; trafficked magical items or ingredients, such as virgin parchment or prophecies; exchanged knowledge; and even shared clients or referred them to each other.

This economy was covert; magicians did not jangle their wares on the street corners. Instead they were sought out for their services in periods of crisis or intrigue. Potential clients found magicians by word of mouth, sometimes (as we will see with William Neville) exerting considerable effort to find the ones with the best reputations. Although it is clear that magicians competed for clients, it is also evident that some magicians knew each other and even exchanged clients. Magicians had differentiated skills or specializations, and these seem to have facilitated cooperation among them. They worked with different sorts of spirits or spiritual mechanisms and offered services ranging from identifying petty thieves to healing to necromantic conjuring. They could also adapt themselves to specific needs.

These active communities seem to stand in opposition to conventional views of magicians and also their literary representations. From Merlin to Dumbledore, magicians have been depicted as celibate hermits who performed most of their significant magical operations by themselves in monastic isolation. This picture has some justification in the magic literature not least due to its clerical origins. The *Ars notoria* requires long periods of isolation and the key rituals must be performed during those times.[21] Similarly, the central ritual in the *Sworn Book of Honorius* (*Liber iuratus Honorii*) purports to provide a solitary vision of the divine.[22] John Steward (see the Mixindale case) also invoked this mythology with his putative quip, "Let God, the devil, and me alone!" by which he meant that he would go off and privately conjure a demon with divine support in order to get the required information about Jameson's servant. However, this was more a matter of bravado than reality. Most of the rituals in the *Sworn Book of Honorius* follow the more conventional

21. For a description of the two-year procedure for the Notory Art, see Julien Véronèse, "Magic, Theurgy, and Spirituality in the Medieval Ritual of the *Ars Notoria*," in *Invoking Angels*, ed. Claire Fanger (University Park: Pennsylvania State University Press, 2012), 37–78.

22. Hedegård, *Liber iuratus Honorii*.

scripts found in necromantic literature, which not only assume the presence of compatriots but give them essential roles in the rituals. The Mixindale Fellowship, which Steward joined, worked together, and members shared responsibilities appropriate to their station: delivering letters and fetching horses, performing religious rites, providing books and practical knowledge, or furnishing material support such as housing. The *Sworn Book* takes this into account in its rules for transmission, which insist on small groups of dependable men tested for their loyalty and sworn to secrecy and mutual protection. The primary failure of the communities examined here (and the reason they got caught) was that they were not as secretive or exclusive as they should have been.

THE CASE OF WILLIAM STAPLETON

The letter of confession written to Cardinal Wolsey in 1528 by the clerical treasure hunter William Stapleton beautifully illustrates much of what we have described here.[23] Stapleton, a Benedictine monk, was tired of being disciplined for sleeping through the morning offices and not performing other duties. He arranged with his superior to have a half-year dispensation from his duties to raise enough money to purchase a full dispensation that would allow him to become a hermit who was in charge of his own schedule. Together with his associate John Kerver, Stapleton had already become involved in magic. He was in possession of magic books, including the *Treasury of Spirits* (*Thesaurus spirituum*), which he had borrowed from another priest. Kerver had also put him in touch with two men, probably William Smith and a man called Amylion, whom Stapleton describes as cunning men.

23. Full transcriptions of both the confession and also documents concerning the activities of William Smith and Amylion may be found in Dawson Turner, "Brief Remarks Accompanied with Documents Illustrative of Trial by Jury, Treasure-Trove, and the Invocation of Spirits for the Discovery of Hidden Treasure in the Sixteenth Century," *Norfolk Archaeology or Miscellaneous Tracts Relating to the Antiquities of the County of Norfolk* 1 (1847): 50–64. See also K. M. Briggs, *The Anatomy of Puck: An Examination of Fairy Beliefs Among Shakespeare's Contemporaries and Successors* (London: Routledge & Kegan Paul, 1959), 255–61.

Smith and Amylion worked for Lord Curzon, who had a license from the crown for treasure hunting, and they seem to have made most of their money not through magic but by fining others who engaged in treasure hunting in their territory without a license. It is likely that they teamed up with Stapleton because, in addition to being a monk, he was an ordained priest and could perform the crucial magical operations that they needed. They provided Stapleton with more books on treasure hunting and together they set about to find hidden gold with the assistance of demons.

The account that Stapleton gives of his career as a magician is extensive and convoluted. He undertook several operations in Norfolk before he began to attract clients from elsewhere, evidently having achieved some notoriety. He made frequent contact with other clerics and cunning men who had been or were still involved in similar activities. During the course of this, he also came into possession of materials for summoning the spirit Oberion, including a circle, sword, and "plate" used for invocations. Other magicians had used them for treasure hunting without success. Although they had managed to conjure the demons, the spirits told them that Oberion was already working for Cardinal Wolsey and therefore could not help them! Although he never found so much as a groat, Stapleton worked in a series of treasure-hunting projects and for a succession of people, including various high-ranking and wealthy patrons, among them Lord Leonard Marquess. Although he failed to find money in Leonard's garden, which the Lord had buried as a test of his skill, Leonard nonetheless bought him a dispensation to become a secular priest and made him his personal chaplain and magician.

Stapleton was finally arrested, but not for treasure hunting. Leonard arranged the arrest because the magician had left his service without permission. Unfortunately, as a result of the arrest, Stapleton's treasure-hunting equipment ended up in the hands of none other than Sir Thomas More, from whom, as far as the records go, he never retrieved it. After Stapleton mended fences with his lord, Leonard secured his release. Had Stapleton been a little more careful, he might well have stayed out of trouble. However, he was drawn back into magic practice, this time by the servants of the Duke of Norfolk. They told Stapleton that the duke believed that Cardinal Wolsey had set an evil spirit on him and needed his help. Although he claimed no expertise in this area, the attraction of such a powerful client must have proved too great and he was convinced to perform magic involving a wax figure to protect the duke. For reasons that are unclear, Stapleton was finally forced by the duke to write the letter of confession to Cardinal Wolsey, perhaps because the duke wanted to publicize Stapleton's claim that the cardinal had bound the spirit Oberion. What happened to Stapleton afterward is unknown, but there is no record of arrest or of ecclesiastical proceedings against him.

The story reveals a good deal about the magic of rogues. Many people were involved in the practice of magic, and there were numerous people willing to pay for such services. Even in the face of strong evidence that the magic did not work, the allure was still powerful. Magicians operated in complex networks in which they exchanged books and information, and even cooperated for periods of time. Finally, magicians tended to come to the attention of the authorities for reasons other than the practice of magic in itself—Stapleton because he *did not* practice magic!—and they often walked free afterward, particularly if they had wealthy and influential clients.

READING AND INTERPRETING LEGAL DOCUMENTS

This volume presents a variety of documents produced when magic practitioners came to the attention of ecclesiastical and secular authorities that we can loosely describe as "legal documents" because they were either assembled in courts or with an eye to potential legal proceedings. In the case of the Yorkshire treasure hunters, the documents were produced by the Archbishop's Court in York. The other materials are not court documents as such but rather the paperwork retained by the crown surrounding various investigations. The documents relating to William Neville's activities, for example, are preserved in the State Papers of Henry VIII and include letters of denunciation, confessions, pleas for leniency, and suchlike. Because they were written in situations where an unguarded word could have dire consequences, they hide as much as they reveal and must be read with considerable care. They are also products of a complicated set of interactions.

First, people potentially in trouble with the authorities adopted particular strategies and postures in what they said or wrote.[24] At some points the accused offered intentionally fuzzy responses or left out critical pieces of information, and at others they provided reams of seemingly irrelevant details. Often they revealed enough that was true to appear credible or even remorseful but simultaneously did their best to avoid incriminating themselves. They may also have adopted different sorts of personae or strategies. William Neville, for example, adopted a position of remorseful self-deprecation accompanied by pleas for mercy. The servant William Wilson in the Mixindale case evidently decided that his best chance for lenience would come through forthright disclosure of everything he knew. Many of the accused had a reasonably good idea of what the law had to say about their behavior, and this stood like a dark shadow in the background of everything they said. The result of all of this is that nothing in the documents can be taken entirely at face value. It was all strategically shaped.

Second, the law and its application were complex. All of the people we examine in this book were patently guilty of practicing magic. But as we have seen, depending on the court and the period, practicing magic might not have been illegal. At the same time, the authorities often had multiple ways of approaching a case to get the desired result. Ultimately, it was not so much a matter of guilt or innocence in a general sense as the degree to which one's behavior fit within the carefully defined categories that purveyors of the law regarded as criminal or sinful and that they had decided to employ. Court officials would press these points at great length. For example, the archbishop of York's commissary was very concerned with whether the magicians had made sacrifices to demons and whether they had "put faith" in these processes. These questions were driven by critical points of canon law and so are worth attending to. At the same time,

24. For discussion of courtroom strategies, see Thomas Cohen, "Three Forms of Jeopardy: Honor, Pain, and Truth-Telling in a Sixteenth-Century Italian Courtroom," *Sixteenth Century Journal* 29, no. 4 (1998); Derek Neal, "Suits Make the Man: Masculinity in Two English Law Courts, c. 1500," *Canadian Journal of History* 37, no. 1 (April 2002): 1–22; Natalie Zemon Davis, *Fiction in the Archives: Pardon Tales and Their Tellers in Sixteenth-Century France*, The Harry Camp Lectures at Stanford University (Stanford: Stanford University Press, 1987).

such concerns can make the sources difficult to use because matters of key interest to modern readers, such as the order of events, might be utterly irrelevant to those who shaped the documents in the first place. Historians are left trying to piece these together as best they can.

EDITORIAL PRINCIPLES

In general, the titles have not been drawn from the original texts. The intended readers of this volume include students and nonspecialists. As a result, the texts have been rendered in English accessible to modern readers, although every attempt has been made to preserve the original words and word order. Otiose occurrences of the word "and" have occasionally been removed for clarity. Some archaic forms (e.g., "saith" versus "says") have been retained, but otherwise punctuation and spelling have been modernized. Where we have translated words, since there was no direct modern English equivalent, the original has been indicated in the notes in italics. Where the archaic usages of modern words are employed, the original word is retained in the text and its meaning indicated in the notes following an equal sign.

Significant portions of chapters 2, 3, and 4 are translations from Latin. Where we have emended errors in the Latin for our translation or where our readings are conjectural or debatable, we have indicated the original Latin in the notes. We have also omitted wherever possible the formulaic and highly repetitive use of *"dictus"* and other similar terms from our translations in chapter 3. In texts using both languages, the points of transition from one to the other have been indicated in the notes. Occasionally, brief Latin formulae, words, or incipits have been preserved in the text and their meanings indicated in the notes, particularly where they were understood as words of power. Readers are reminded that the Vulgate numbering of the Psalms differs from modern numbering.

Lacunae or illegible sections of the original manuscript and conjectural readings of such sections have been indicated in angle brackets (e.g., bl<ack>).

PART 1

Magic and the Secular Authorities

CHAPTER 1

William Neville and His Magicians

The Legal Documents

William Neville is remembered as a minor poet of the early sixteenth century for his work *The Castell of Pleasure,* in which the main character, Desire, is led to a castle in a dream vision. Here he encounters various allegorical figures with whom he disputes on the topic of love. The poem concludes with lamentations on the fickleness of fate.[1] A little more than a decade later, fate did turn on Neville and he suffered an inglorious fall from grace for his involvement in magic, necromancy, prophecy, and treason. But it was his desire for money, power, and advancement rather than love that drew him in. Remarkably, a key point in his seduction into the world of magic was a magically induced dream vision of a castle. Neville seems to have been a better soothsayer than a poet and had a better instinct for foretelling his own future than the four magicians he employed. Almost none of *their* predictions played out, even with this kind of eerie irony.

The story of William Neville's legal troubles illustrates the seductive mythology of magic and how magic can be thought of as an expression of anxiety or desire. It also dramatically demonstrates the reality that magic practitioners tended to walk free from encounters with secular authorities, even when they were patently guilty of crimes that fell within the legal definition of treason: foretelling the death of the king, predicting dynastic wars, spreading rumors about this, and assembling resources for military action should they come to pass. If crown officials had been primed to attack magic, these kinds

1. The work was first published when William Neville was only twenty-one. William Neville, *The Castell of Pleasure . . . : The Text of the First Issue of the Poem, with Variant Readings from the Reprint of 1518,* edited by Roberta D. Cornelius (Oxford: Oxford University Press for the Early English Text Society, 1930).

PEOPLE INVOLVED IN THE CASE

TABLE 1: List of People in the William Neville Case

The Nevilles

William	Second son of Richard Neville, Second Baron Latimer
Elizabeth	Wife of William Neville
Christopher	One of William's younger brothers
George	One of William's younger brothers
John	Third Baron Latimer and William's older brother

Friends and servants of William Neville

Thomas Wood	Gentleman and associate of William Neville
Edward Legh	A priest and chaplain to William Neville
Thomas Avinell	A priest and chaplain to William Neville
John Latemore	Servant
Roger Winter John Walsh William Gower of Worcestershire Richard Sheldon John Morgan of Worcestershire	Associates that William Neville named as officers to serve under him should he become an Earl

Cunning men and their servants

Richard Jones of Oxford	Magician and alchemist at Oxford
Tyler	Servant to Richard Jones
William Wade	A cunning man hired by William Neville described as "a Kalcar* or a wise man among common people"
Nash of Cirencester	Cunning man and associate of Richard Jones
Hurlock	Probably William Harlock (aka Old Hurlock), detained in 1530 for his prophetic calendar
Master Hugh	Cunning man from Staffordshire

Others

Robert Webb	Yeoman of the King's studs

*= a diviner or cunning man

of activities would be low-hanging fruit. However, if Henry VIII's 1542 legislation were a sign of building administrative concern with magic, that concern was nowhere evident in this case less than ten years before.

STORY SUMMARY[2]

William Neville of Penwyn, Worcestershire (now Pinvin), was born in 1497, the second son of the twelve children (six sons and six daughters) of Richard Neville, second Baron Latimer (ca. 1467–1530).[3] As was common practice for noble youths, William spent time serving in a great household; based on his confession and the comments of others William served for a time in the household of Cardinal Wolsey. From 1524 onward he held various local offices, such as the commissioner of the peace for Worcester.[4] Sometime before 1529 William Neville had married Elizabeth, daughter of Sir Giles Greville. The couple had three children. The bulk of his estates in Gloucester and Worcester came to him through his marriage; some others he inherited directly. William's older brother John succeeded their father in 1530 to become the third Baron Latimer.

Primogeniture meant that second and subsequent sons of nobles had very different lives from their eldest brothers. Their fortunes often depended on the wealth of their mother's family, judicious marriages, and luck. For many the pressure to maintain the wealth and status into which they were born was the source of considerable anxiety. This was perhaps more poignant for second sons who were only one or two untimely deaths away from greatness. William's brother and nephew were all that separated him from becoming Lord Latimer. Importantly for this story, he could also trace his lineage back to Warwick the

2. Our summary builds upon the discussion of this case in Elton, *Policy and Police*, 49–57.

3. Arthur Collins, *Collin's Peerage of England*, 9 vols. (n.p., 1812), 5:155.

4. A. S. G. Edwards, "Neville, William (b. 1497, d. in or before 1545), poet," in *Oxford Dictionary of National Biography* (hereafter DNB), http://www.oxforddnb.com/view/10.1093/ref:odnb/9780198614128.001.0001/odnb-9780198614128-e-19968.

Kingmaker, Richard Neville the sixteenth Earl of Warwick, although the title had not been bestowed since 1499. Thus, it was not completely inconceivable that William Neville might believe he could receive that title. The magic practitioners and purveyors of prophecies who preyed upon his pocketbook no doubt knew he was tantalizingly close to considerably greater status and wealth.

It all began in December 1531 when William Neville consulted Nash, a cunning man, about some stolen spoons. Perhaps sensing the opportunities offered by a comparatively wealthy and credulous client, Nash quickly seems to have started offering predictions about William's future. William's wife, Elizabeth, would die. He would then marry a young and wealthy heiress and succeed his brother to the title of Lord Latimer within five years. Nash also spoke highly of a more scholarly cunning man and medical practitioner, Richard Jones of Oxford. Putatively seeking help for his wife's illness, Neville invited Jones to his home and on that visit Jones confirmed Nash's prediction of future greatness. He added that Elizabeth would live no longer than ten more years, after which he would marry a very young heiress who would bring him five hundred marks of land. In the meantime, Jones offered to make William a magical device to ensure the favor of his brother.

Shortly after this, William and his younger brother George visited Jones in Oxford. Jones evidently impressed William with his scholarly comportment, claims to high connections, and rooms full of magic books, magical tools, and alchemical equipment. Jones also expanded upon his predictions, claiming that he had experienced a dream vision in which a spirit led him into a high tower where William was presented with coats of arms signaling that he had been made an earl. Thomas Wood (William's associate) claimed this vision was brought on by necromantic magic, which seems credible. They then determined to go to Warwick Castle to assure that this was the place in the dream. This trip took place on September 29, 1532, and Jones confirmed that Warwick was indeed the castle in his dream. During their visit, an old man also approached them in the town, welcoming William back "to his own." One suspects Jones may have set this meeting up in advance, but with some encouragement, William evidently took it as a sign from God that he would possess the castle. On the ride home, Jones elaborated upon the events at Warwick, claiming to have fought a battle with a spirit on William's behalf. He also warned that there would be a battle before All Hallows' Eve in which William's older brother would die and that William should be ready to ride immediately to the house to secure the finances.

As compelling as the evidence may have been to him, William still harbored doubts. He sought out other cunning men to confirm the predictions. One William Wade assured him that he would become earl. Another cunning man whom he sought out, called Hurlock, turned out to be dead and unable to help. Finally, yet another, named Master Hugh, cautiously advised that William would not be a lord for a long time and that he should take no action. In addition to these consultations, William also sought for confirmation in prophetic texts. These texts were provided by his servant, Thomas Wood, and the cunning men whom he consulted. These texts seemed to confirm the predictions of Nash, Jones, and Wade, and William began to openly fantasize about how wonderful it would be to have a house near London. In the coming weeks he also discussed what offices his friends and servants would take up under his patronage. Sometime during this period, he tried his own hand at magic, using a magic book that he owned. He sent his long-suffering chaplain Edward Legh on a long quest to find materials to make a cloak of invisibility.[5] The results of this experiment are not known, but it seems likely that after failing to make himself vanish, he either pursued his efforts at magic privately or decided to leave magic in the hands of hired professionals.

From the moment William had begun to engage with magicians who predicted the death of a peer of the realm (i.e., his brother), he was straying into dangerous legal territory, which became increasingly more dangerous as the predictions and advice from Nash and Jones stretched to involve King Henry VIII.[6] Following their trip to Warwick Castle, William, his younger brother Christopher, and Thomas Wood made a trip to William's property at Wick and on the way lodged with

5. The details and many ambiguities of this case have been more fully summarized in Elton, *Policy and Police*, 49–57.

6. Edward Legh claims that Neville and members of his household hypothetically discussed the use of poison, but not that there were any plans to use it. See Text 1.1.

Nash. The cunning man predicted a period of political and military instability and the imminent death of the king. According to Wood, William believed that Henry VIII would die in France and this would be followed by a Scottish invasion. Apparently, Nash was in possession of a convincing prophetic text that supported his prediction.

The reader will find a good deal of uncomfortable finger pointing in the participants' narratives at this point. When Henry VIII actually departed for Calais on October 11, 1532, William posted a man in London to deliver news about the king. According to Legh and Wood, he began to make preparations to leap into the predicted political and military chaos of a succession crisis. Wood claims that William sought out allies with ready cash, which he could use to support a group of armed retainers. William's counterclaim that Wood had counseled him to seek out loans from the Abbot of Pershore and the Parson of Fladbury[7] only served to demonstrate that Wood may have actively participated in these problematic discussions. Although it seems doubtful that he could have done it in the time between Nash's first prediction and his arrest, Wood also says William expanded his gallery to accommodate such a military force. Whatever the truth of the matter may have been, William and his accomplices had stumbled into the territory of treason by openly discussing the death of the king. The ring that Jones delivered to William around this time was clearly meant to magically induce favor from superiors and this verged on treason as well. With all of this in play, things began to unravel.

By William's account his good relations with Thomas Wood had begun to deteriorate before Henry VIII returned from France on November 14, 1532, after which it became increasingly obvious that the predictions would not come true. In his confession William implied that there was a longstanding tension between them over William's unwillingness to take on Wood as a member of his household or to promise him the position of Master of the Buckhounds after he became earl. Naturally, William may have concocted these stories to draw doubt upon his accuser's credibility. As Christmas approached,

7. Pershore was about a kilometer northwest from Wick and Fladbury, less than four kilometers as the crow flies to the east, somewhat farther if traveling along the Avon.

William's chaplain, Edward Legh, was evidently becoming increasingly worried about his master's activities as well. Perhaps motivated by the fact that the king was very much still alive, Legh and Wood decided to go public together. In December, Legh wrote to the king's Privy Council to spill the beans.

Thomas Cromwell acted quickly and had many of the key people rounded up, including William Neville, his brother George, and Richard Jones. Edward Legh (Text 1.1) and Thomas Wood (Text 1.2) made full statements on December 30. Richard Jones's servant Roger Tyler was apprehended in early January (Text 1.9).[8] No mention is made of Nash and Wade having been apprehended, despite the fact that they certainly would have been persons of interest in this case. They seem to have disappeared, possibly having gotten wind of the arrests. What Cromwell thought of all this is unclear, but it is certain that things could have gone much worse for William, George, Tyler, and Jones.

In the end, as Geoffrey Elton dryly notes, they were "more fortunate than their idiocy deserved," and they all walked free.[9] Remarkably in 1534, William appealed to Cromwell that he had been impoverished by his recent troubles. Cromwell intervened on his behalf with the Abbess of Wilton, referring to him as a friend. William ended up being awarded several minor offices from the crown in later years.[10] Tyler, Wood, Nash, and Wade all vanish from the record. Legh complained in 1533 to Cromwell that he had not been discharged from the requirement that he had to stay in attendance as an accuser (Text 1.8), but no response survives.

Jones remained in the Tower of London for some time.[11] In his second letter (Text 1.6), he shamelessly offered the crown his services as

---

8. Although Geoffrey Elton suggests that The National Archives of the United Kingdom (henceforth TNA) SP 1/73/3 was a letter from Tyler to Jones, the internal evidence is unconvincing, so we have not included it with the transcribed texts here. The intended recipient of the letter was a priest in service to the king. Jones was neither. Elton, *Policy and Police*, 55.

9. Ibid.

10. Neville, *Castell of Pleasure . . .* , 70–71. For his letter to Cromwell on his impoverishment, see *Letters and Papers, Foreign and Domestic* (hereafter *LP*), *Henry VIII*, vol. 7, 1649. For Cromwell's intervention for his friend William Neville, see *LP Henry VIII*, vol. 11, 271.

11. At some point his brother, Roger Jones, wrote to Cromwell to ask for his release. See TNA SP 1/238.

an alchemist along with incriminating information about Dr. London of New College.[12] Although it suggests a remarkable level of bravado, this letter may also have been written at a time when he had reason to hope for safe release. In the same letter he says that the Earl of Worcester and Sir William Morgan would speak on his behalf, and it may be the latter who secured his release. Elton notes that Jones may have been involved in a robbery in 1535 in Oxford, but no Jones seems to have been punished for that offense.[13]

The outcome illustrates the curious disinclination of secular courts to prosecute crimes of magic. The magic itself was not a crime under common law at that time, but there was plenty of evidence that could have allowed Cromwell to proceed against William and his accomplices had there been any desire to do so. William's confession might also have confirmed what Cromwell already thought: that the nobleman had been stupid and gullible and had already been sufficiently shamed by his arrest that no further punishment was necessary. Jones's influential patrons, who probably had employed him for magic themselves, may have helped him evade further punishment. Whatever the reasons for Cromwell's lack of further action, those reasons evidently outweighed any personal desire or institutional pressure to prosecute magicians and their employers.

PROPHECY

The prophetic texts mentioned in this case belong to a complicated and long-standing tradition of political prophecy in medieval England and in particular to a subset of prophecy about northern magnates in the fifteenth century.[14] The "child with a chaplet" prophecy mentioned by

12. John London, Warden of New College, Oxford, and an associate of Thomas Cromwell. See H. L. Parish, "London, John (1485/6–1543), Administrator," *Oxford Dictionary of National Biography*. September 23, 2004. https://doi.org/10.1093/ref:odnb/16957.

13. Elton, *Policy and Police*, 56.
14. Lesley A. Coote, *Prophecy and Public Affairs in Later Medieval England* (York: York Medieval Press, 2000). On the "Erceldoune" prophecies and northern magnates, see 231.

Neville was almost certainly from the third section of "The Prophisies of Rymour, Beid, and Marlyng," which begins:

> A child with a chaplet shall raye hym right
> with many a hardy man of hande
> with many a helme that clyderith bright
> And he shall com ouer the soelway sand;
> on standys more begyn to fight
> where lordes shall light vpon that londe,
> And ask Nothing but his Right
> yet shall his enymys hym with stand.[15]

The child goes on to conquer England and become king. Neville and his compatriots quite reasonably followed the common interpretation of this text as foretelling the invasion of England by a Scottish king.[16] The forces that contend with each other during this invasion are represented as animals, including a dragon, wolf, swan, bear, and others. The bear and ragged staff were the badge of Richard Neville, Earl of Warwick, in the fifteenth century and thus reasonably associated with the Neville family in general.[17] William Neville also had another prophecy in his possession in which "a beyr whiche had ben long tyde to a stake shuld arise and make peace & vnytie." He took this to mean that he, as a Neville, would accede to the position of Earl of Warwick, last held by his family in the fifteenth century. It has been suggested that he regarded this as a prediction that he would be a successful rebel against Henry VIII (taken to be the dragon), but even Neville's accuser, Wood, makes it clear that Neville and his associates assumed that the invasion would take place in the chaos *after* the king's death in France.[18]

15. I quote from the edition of the text in James A. H. Murray, *The Romance and Prophecies of Thomas of Erceldonne Printed from Five Manuscripts; with Illustrations from the Prophetic Literature of the 15th and 16th Centuries*, Early English Text Society (London: Trubner, 1875), 56 (lines 301–8).

16. Sharon L. Jansen Jaech, "The 'Prophisies of Rymour, Beid, and Marlyng': Henry VIII and a Sixteenth-Century Political Prophecy," *Sixteenth Century Journal* 16, no. 3 (1985): 291–300.

17. Coote, *Prophecy and Public Affairs*, 198.

18. Jaech, "'Prophisies of Rymour, Beid, and Marlyng,'" 298.

Medieval and early modern manuscripts of magic rarely include prophecies, perhaps indicating that the practitioners of magic and the peddlers of prophecy were distinct groups. However, the case of William Neville suggests these groups were rather more familiar with one another's trade or were even sometimes the same people. As we have seen, William employed his cunning men as magic practitioners, but he also employed them to divine the future through magic and to find and interpret prophecies. Nash and Richard Jones, who knew each other, served in both roles. Evidence suggests that Richard Jones was also familiar with Hurlock, whom Neville hoped to consult but discovered to be dead (Texts 1.1 and 1.3). Sharon Jansen has suggested that one William Harlock, detained in 1530 for writing a prophetic calendar, and "old Hurlock," mentioned in other documents in connection with prophecy, were the same person. This William Harlock mentioned having met with one Richard Jones.[19] The circumstantial evidence for an extended network of magicians and prophesiers including Jones, Nash, and Hurlock is thus significant. Certainly, for potential patrons like William Neville, magicians and prophesiers could serve the same purpose, and at least in the 1530s, practitioners were willing to turn a hand to either practice.

THE TEXTS

1.1. Statement of Edward Legh from Papers of Thomas Cromwell December 1532[20]

Note: Sections of this document are very badly damaged. Gaps in the text due to mutilation and speculative readings of the missing text are indicated in angle brackets.

The 8th day of October at South Cerney, my master William Neville called me to him in the morning before day, before his brother Christopher Neville and Thomas Wood, gentleman. He asked my counsel

19. Jansen, *Political Protest and Prophecy*, 27–28.

20. TNA E 163 10/20

to have gone to one Hurlock, a kalcar[21] dwelling in War<mins>tar in
the County of Wilton, because he wanted to know how the end of
getting the Earldom of Warwick should speed[22] for he had <been>
at Warwick before with certain of his council and servants to view
the castle and there was one by the way [who] inquired of one of his
servants what gentleman his master was and he said he was Master
William Neville of W<ick . . . and he> said that he was welcome to his
own for it w<. . .> [23]Earl of Warwick so forth <. . .> his servant <. . .>
commanded the man to come to his inn <. . .> and he would none
but was gone suddenly and he <did not> see him after. Wherefore he
thought it came of God. I said it was a marvelous thing and showed him
that if Hurlock were alive, he could show him many things touching
the Earldom of Warwick or anything else as I had heard before. So,
he commanded me to call up his servants. Then it was showed him
that Hurlock was dead, whereupon he tarried, etc.

Also, at the same time he sent one Sir[24] Thomas Avenell, a young
priest into Gloucestershire to fetch a man to him that had many prophesies, and if he could not bring him, to send him his books or else to
copy forth such things as were most for his purpose. The priest brought
him the copy of such a prophecy as he thought best by his discretion.

Also, at his coming home he fetched forth a book and let me see
the arms of my ancestries and the name of the head house thereof and
said it was the greatest name among gentlemen in England. He told me
that he that could make most friends should speed best, for the King's
Grace would go over the sea, and my Lady Marquise of Pembroke[25]
with his Grace, and there they should be married, and that the French
king would not meet him and the King's Grace should not reign fully
the space of 24 years, but be slain, and none of his blood should reign
after him, and that the realm should be long without a king and that
he that were of great blood should have all the rule of the realm and

21. = a diviner or cunning man

22. *<how it?> shuld spede as an
endes the yeorldome of Warwycke*

23. The MS is quite damaged in this
spot and has a large hole in the middle
of it. Each gap (indicated by angle
brackets) may have included between
three and six words.

24. = Father. The title Sir (*Dominus*) was frequently used for parsons
prior to the Reformation and does
not mean the priest was a knight, as it
would mean for non-clerical men also
addressed as Sir. We retain the title
here and throughout.

25. Anne Boleyn.

subdue those that the King had made of low blood[26] and that there should have been fought three fields[27] in England before Christmas day and the child with a chaplet should reign and rule the realm, which as he named, should be the Scottish king.

Also, he fetched forth after that time another book and let me see a conceit, as he called it, for to make him a privy coat because he dared not trust his servants to do it. It was bones of horse shins and chalk and rosin and powder of glass and I could find but one horse leg though I looked for dead horses every day and all other things were ready. The coat should be made of linen cloth and a buckskin in the middle thereof. It should be made after that manner that a man might ride or go it and not be spied.

Also, he showed me that the first promotion that he would give spiritual[28] should be unto his brother George Neville and then to his own chaplains and would have had Sir Thomas Avinell to wait on his wife when I should have ridden with him [i.e., Neville] into the north—and he promised him to do so. When he sent for him again, he [i.e., Avinell] sent him short words not to his pleasure that [he] would not be there as he should do so great reverence, and if the priest [i.e., Avinell] be examined I think he will show his mind.[29]

Also, he sent me for one William Wade, called a Kalcar or a wise man among common people, and I went for him to Pyrton and he was gone to Elmley with a gentleman. Then he caused me to ride for him in the night to have conveyed him [Wade] thither secretly and he was gone thence. When I came home and showed him, he [Neville] took me into his privy gallery and told me that he [Wade] had put him in comfort of the Earldom of Warwick and that he said he should be Lord Latimer for he [the current Lord] should be slain with Scots. He bade me take company with me and if he [Wade] should not come by fair means, that I should cause the constable to take him and bring him before him for he would lay such things to his charge as should teach

26. I.e., those whom the king had raised from low estate to high positions.

27. = battles

28. I.e., the first spiritual office he would grant.

29. The upshot of this tortured passage is that Avinell had a falling out with Neville and might be willing to serve as a witness for the crown.

all the traitors in England to take example of him. In the morning he
lent me his wife's nag and sent one of his servants with me (at my own
choosing, for I thought to have him that I thought would abide) and
his brother Christopher lent me his sword. When I came to Pyrton I
found him [Wade] at Master Foliatte's and made his brother to go to
him and he was loath to come. Then at last I said that I would have him
broken or whole, knowing the cause touching treason,[30] and at the last
he came with me and his brother with him and was welcome to my
master as any man, and I thought he [Neville] would have attached[31]
him. Then my master gave him a doublet of silk and a nightcap of
velvet and a hat when he departed from him.

Also, as we rode betwixt Cirencester and Hailes, talking of these
kalcars, I asked him how they had such knowledge that had no learning. He showed me that Nash had his knowledge by familiarity with a
spirit. I asked him whether he did any sacrifice and he said he must give
the spirit something and [likewise] every man that had his knowledge
of them. He said that Wade had his knowledge of the fairies and he had
made them [a] promise that he would meddle in no thing of longer time
than from New Year's Day till New Year's Day, nor would [he] at no
time, for he had proved him many times.[32] Then I showed him of one
Master Hugh that had lain long in an abbey in the County of Stafford
called duly Eucrast otherwise called delecryse [i.e., Dieulacres Abbey]
and there he had shown many things both of change of weather and
of things to be found under the earth. He asked me whether he could
tell any things concerning the promotion of noble men of blood, and
I said I thought he could, for he would tell a man how he should speed
in his matters and the law that was a suitor,[33] as I had been informed.
He asked me whether he were there still, and I said, "No. He lay at
Lenton beside Nottingham at Master John Delapare's house, the which
was a physician." Then he was desirous to go to him or to devise by
his [Neville's] mind and mine some way that might cause him [Master

---

30. I.e., knowing that the cause of
Neville summoning him concerned
treason.

31. *tachyd*—i.e., arrested.

32. The meaning of much of this
passage is unclear, but the final phrase

evidently means that Neville knew the
foregoing because he had proved (i.e.,
tested) Wade many times.

33. I.e., and how someone bringing
suit should fare in a legal case.

Hugh] to come over to him. Then he beat upon that journey for such a long time that I was daily afraid on my head if it should be known,[34] and I was sick. When I was whole he still wanted to go or to send me to him, and one day when he was ridden from home, I went forth all that day, and at night when he had come home, I came home after him, and showed him that, by chance, I fortuned to meet with Master Hugh and that he and I fell into communication of him, and that he said that he knew his arms, and that he [Neville] should be master a great while before he should be a lord, and that he should not make any[35] friends, nor stir himself till he were called upon. Then we kept the gallery still daily in communication whether he was gone or when he would come again, and I said he [Neville] could not tell but that he should make no labor to him to no place until he came himself.[36] Then he caused me to tarry at Parsear bridge[37] both before noon and after at dinner time and to send unto Robert French['s] wife that, if he [Master Hugh] came, he should tarry, for my master would either come to him or send for him by me. At the last, he [Neville] saw that he would not come and desired me to make a letter to him. I said I would and because I dared not write a secret letter that should not be known about such a matter (for he would tarry no longer because the King's Grace was forth of his realm and should not come again as he said, and the scots were busy according to his prophecy) I wrote the letter to the Prior of Lenton, praying him that one of his servants might commendeth the bearer of it unto Master Hugh to speak with him for certain matters the which I would show him of at the next time that I spoke with him. The letter went forth with one John Lamb, that is his secret messenger, and then the man was dead.[38]

In the mean time, Master Wood withdrew him[self] from his [Neville's] favor and I came to him and desired him of his counsel for I say he [Neville] went so far without any stop. I showed Master Wood that my friends had done service to all the kings that were of his

<hr />

34. I.e., Legh was concerned he was engaging in traitorous behavior.
35. no
36. I.e., they should make no effort to find Hugh but simply wait until he came to them.

37. Likely Pershore Bridge, now Pershore Old Bridge
38. Presumably, Master Hugh.

blood before his Grace and unto his Grace too, and that I had done his Grace service myself, and [I] have a brother that does his grace service daily, and besides that I was [a] curate at all times since I was a priest. I have read the general sentence of times wherein I have read that all traitors to the King or keepers of their counsel should be accursed. Whereas he [Wood] and I knew his [Neville's] counsel, both that he [Wood] would utter it for the discharge of us both and send for me where or before whom he would, and I would confess the truth so far as I knew of a surety.[39]

Thereupon it was disclosed by a letter of my own hand, writing the 24th day of December unto the King's Honorable Council and the bearer thereof was John Hancocks, Yeoman of the Guard to his noble Grace. God save the King.

Also, another time at supper before his wife, his brother Christopher, and Master Wood, he talked of these calkars.[40] Then I said, "Sir, I do not trust unto such things, for you know very well what great men have lost their lives for such great presumption. Sure, if you do not speed well, it will cost you your head." He said, "No, no. Though one miss, another may prove."[41]

Also, we talked of poison, what should be the conveying most privily thereof. I asked whether it was not treason, by Act of Parliament. He said yes, but it might be conveyed privily diverse ways, and one way was when a priest said grace, he might let it fall when he said grace from betwixt his fingers. However,[42] he named no man that should be so served but by estimation,[43] because he trusted on the death of Lord Latimer.

Written by the hand of me, Sir Edward Legh, 30th day of December in the 24th year of the reign of King Henry VII.[44] All the articles in this book I will be ready to justify when so ever it shall please the King's Grace that I shall be called thereto.

---

39. I.e., Wood would report Neville for both of their sake's and Legh would confess what he knew.
40. = diviner, caster of horoscopes
41. = be successful.
42. *how be hyt*
43. I.e., the discussion was hypothetical.
44. The date is not clear. It could also be December 25.

1.2. Statement of Thomas Wood, December 1532[45]

Accusations declared by Thomas Wood, gentleman, against William Neville 30th day of December, in the 24th year [of the reign of Henry VIII].

First, he says that William showed him that he should be Earl of Warwick and he [Thomas Wood] demanding how he knew that, was answered by William Neville that one Jones of Oxford had, by his cunning, raised four devils which brought the said Jones into a Tower and showed him there the picture of William Neville standing in a robe of velvet and a crown on his head and said it was he that should be Earl of Warwick. Wherunto Thomas Wood advised him to give no trust thereto, for devils would lie, to which William Neville answered, "Nay, doubt not that, for Master Jones and such as have cunning will so bind them that they shall not lie."

Item[46] he said further that William Neville showed him another time, that at this past Michelmas he had been at Warwick and viewed the Castle there. At his coming thither, there met with him an aged man who[47] inquired of his servants what he was. They answered that his name was Master William Neville to which the old man said he was welcome to his own. Thereupon, with great reverence, [he] came to William Neville and bade him welcome to his own, for he was, and should be, very Lord there. To which, Thomas Wood said, "Trust no such sayings. Belike it was a poor man that thereby procured your alms or else some relief of meat or drink." He [Neville] said, "nay" for he never saw him before, nor[48] after.

Item he saith also that William Neville showed him that the King's Highness would shortly [go] over sea and that he should never come again [172v] nor should not reign the full of twenty-three years, and that he knew well by diverse prophesies. He said also that before this feast of Christmas the King of Scots should make three battles in England and should come in by Worcester and obtain.[49] He would

---

45. TNA SP 1/72/172r–174r
46. = also
47. *which*

48. *ne*
49. = be victorious

be at some of these battles himself for he had one [who] would show him when time should be best and who should obtain, to whom he would give faith[50] and be retained.

Item Thomas Wood saith that another season William asked him who should be of his counsel and offices being Earle of Warwick. Whereunto he [Thomas Wood] said he [William Neville] knew that best himself. Then William Neville named Roger Winter, John Walsh, William Gower, sad[51] gentlemen of Worcestershire, and one Richard Sheldon to be his officers and of his counsel, and one John Morgan, a sad gentleman of that shire to be marshal of the hall, and Thomas Wood to be master of his buckhounds and of his parks. Then William Neville was demanded by Thomas how he should come by that Earldom, by the King's gift or otherwise. It was answered by William Neville, "Nay, not by the king, for he shall not reign, but by my right inheritance." To this Thomas said, "My Lord Latymer then should have it before you." "Nay," said he, "My brother shall be slain at one of the said battles, and then shall I have the ward of his son and have both his lands and the Earldom of Warwick." Thomas further saith that William Neville, through[52] all the time the King's Highness was last beyond the sea, had a servant of his, named John Lamb, laying at London for news, whereby he might set forward his evil purpose in so much as, by a fortnight after the King's Highness had arrived [in] this his realm, he [Neville] would [173r] have laid wagers that his grace was not come nor should not return into this Realm.[53] Therefore [he] desired Thomas Wood to help to get him men, for he that had strength should rule— namely he being of great blood—and subdue all others risen by the King's preferment. [He] said he should lack no good, for such as had substance would be fain to bring it to him to be favored and borne.[54] Therefore [he] advised and counseled Thomas Wood to sell his corn and goods and make money and to sow no corn this year—"for them that sow corn shall not reap it this year and money should be ready

50. *leyue*
51. = solemn
52. by
53. I.e., even after Henry actually had returned from France, Neville

remained convinced that he had (and would) not come back.
54. I.e., given his position of power, people would be glad to come to him for favors and he would lack for nothing.

treasure in this season." To which Thomas said, "If I should sell my corn and not keep my seed-time, my wife and children should starve and perish this next year." "Nay," said William Neville, "If you have money you shall be meet[55] to serve me and attain promotions by me and for lack of money you may therein hinder yourself."

Item Thomas Wood saith that a simple person, one Wade, was called by William Neville to labor in astronomy for him, which [Wade] said that Neville should, within this five years, be Earl of Warwick. Thomas Wood saith William Neville resorted much unto and keepeth about him this Wade with others taking it upon them[selves] to be soothsayers[56] and hath so used himself since midsummer and before. Further, Thomas Wood saith that William Neville showed to him a letter and read it to him, which was sent from Jones with the highest style and [173v] recommendation that he ever heard, which said that he [Jones] was not worthy to write to his excellence, and endorsed it to the Right Honorable William Neville, Earl of Warwick et cetera.

Item furthermore William Neville showed unto Thomas Wood that a bear which had been long tied to a stake should arise and make peace and unity. Thomas Wood demanded [of] him who was the bear and William Neville named himself the bear and Earle of Warwick.

Item after Thomas Wood says that William Neville showed him that one Nash, being a calkar, said that he should be Earl of Warwick and that he would jeopard[57] his life thereupon. Further [he] said that he should have all the lands of the Earldom of Warwick in his hands and said that he should be much desirous to lie in a place of the Earl of Warwick being beside London near about the Thames side and bade him inquire at London for the same place, etc. [174r].

Item Thomas Wood saith that William Neville said unto to him that he should find great treasure in the Castle of Warwick. Thomas demanded how that might be. To that William answered and said that when the Earl of Warwick went to battle, he hid his treasure in a tower of the same castle. William Neville said that he should translate[58] and

55. = ready
56. *whiche Wade with others takyng vpon them to be soth sayers the said Thomas wood saith that the said*
William nevyll resortithe muche vnto and kepith aboute him
57. = wager
58. = move

build the same castle anew and then, by means thereof, he should find the same treasure so hid etc.

Item also Thomas Wood saith that William Neville showed him that he made his new gallery at Wick to and for the intent [that] he might keep therein one or two hundred men at his need, and hath made draw doors and other privy doors to convey the same number of men at his pleasure, etc.

by me Thomas Wood

1.3. Confession of William Neville[59]

Memorandum that I William Neville before Christmas was twelve-month,[60] having other business into those parts, did send John Lamb, my servant, to one Nash of Cirencester. Forsomuch as one chamber of London where I was lodged, said he [i.e., John Lamb], missed certain spoons which were delivered to my servants, so I sought to know from him [Nash] where they were. He said the chamber missed none and further said that he knew more concerning me than I did myself, both concerning Lashborow and other [things]. He said [if] I would give him a try[61] he would tell me many things which should chance to me of profit. After that he sent a letter, and the effect thereof was this: be ye merry; thy son shall inherit all except Lasheborow, for he shall be my lord your brother's heir. Then I sent for the said Nash in Lent and in my garden at Wick he said my master's, your wife, shall not live long, although she is at this hour as hardy whole as any woman in England. But you shall have another wife by whom ye shall have much land, who shall be of the Graystokes kindred and you shall be Lord Latimer about five years hence. But before that you shall have the wardship of your nephew, which you shall buy and after forego him and he shall not live long after.[62] After that [Nash] sent me word that within eighteen months a thing[63] should chance to me that should be

59. TNA SP 1/72/175r–178v
60. I.e., before last Christmas.
61. *tree*

62. I.e., he would purchase the wardship from the crown and ultimately supersede his nephew as heir.
63. *thi<ng>*

profitable. After, my brother George came to me from Oxford, and when he heard me speak of the same Nash, he desired to speak with him. So, he, my brother Christopher, and I rode thither. At which time, Nash praised much one Jones in Oxford and showed me a letter that he [Jones] had written to him, desirous to be acquainted with the abbot then of Cirencester, promising to do him great pleasure, Nash affirming that Jones had more cunning than him, and praising him as a good physician. For which reason, my wife being sick, I sent for him to Oxford a good while after, and he came. I asked him how long he thought my wife might live, seeing he said her life would be short, and he said ten years she might be patched forth[64] but no longer [175r], wherein I desired him to do the best he could. Then he told me that I should have a young wife that should not pass 15 years old at the marriage and I should have by her 500 marks [of] land and also that I should be Lord Latimer and that I should be greater than a Baron. As I remember at that time, he said he would make a thing for me by means whereof my lord my brother should favor me above all men, which should take effect before All Hallows' Tide, for which purpose he said he would devise two faces[65] and tell me how I should order them. Because he told me at our next meeting that my lord, my brother, should live so short a while as is written hereafter, we had no more communication thereof since that time. So [Jones] departed for Oxford again, and because my brother George sent me word to reward him largely, I gave him twenty shillings because he promised to do my wife great good and me great pleasure.

After that I went to Oxford, intending that my brother George and I should kill a buck with Sir Simon de Harcourt, which he had promised me. There at Oxford, in the said Jones's chamber, [I] did see certain stillatories, alembics, and other instruments of glass, a scepter and other things, which he said appertained to the conjuration of the four kings, and also an image of white metal, and in a box a serpent's skin as he said, and diverse books and things whereof one was a book, which he said was my lord Cardinal's, having pictures in it like angels.

---

64. I.e., she might live on with a patchwork of care.

65. Meaning unclear. Possibly "images" or "decans," both of which suggests astrological images.

He told us that he could make rings of gold to obtain favor of great men and said that my Lord Cardinal had such, and promised either my brother and me, either of us, one of them. He also showed me a round thing like a ball of crystal.

Also, he said that if the King's Grace went over[seas], his grace should marry my Lady Marquise of Pembroke before that his highness returned again and that it would be dangerous to his grace and to the most part of the noble men that went with his highness. He supposed that my lord my brother should go in that journey saying also that he had written to one of the King's council to advise his highness not to go over, for if he did it would not be for his grace's profit [176r].

Also, in a morning at Oxford, Jones asked me whether the gold and azure check with a chevron of ermine was given in the arms of our ancestors. I told him that the Lord Latimer did give it as common of one of the daughters and heirs of Sir Richard Beauchamp, sometime Earl of Warwick. Whereunto he said that the spirit came to him uncalled, having such arms in his hand, and led him by the hand up into a high tower. There in the highest chamber, he delivered the same arms to me. For which cause he said he would gladly <go to> the Castle of Warwick to know if it were the same or no, and that my brother George and he would come to me and go to see it at Michaelmas. [They] came and thither I went with them, and after the sight of much of the fairest [parts] of the castle, went up into the high chamber of the tower on the right hand of the coming in into the castle. He said that that was it, showing me there a circle, saying that there had been used conjurations sometime.[66] On the morrow, in the town of Warwick after mass, an old man met me in the street and bade me welcome to my own. I answered that I was but a poor man and not <likely> that & so he went his way, wither nor what he was I <know> not. In our riding homewards I asked Jones what he thought and he said that it was told him beyond the sea by a cunning man that he should be chief counsel with one that should be a great man of the realm. This he ascribed to <me> and said I should be Earl of Warwick.

66. I.e., that magic had been performed there.

He said also that there should be a field in the north soon <after>
All Hallows Tide in the borders, in which he said my lord brother
should be slain. He bade me be in readiness to ride thither for he
would find the means that I should be there after[wards], as my lady
sister should know of it and have much of that money that was my
lord father's, which he said lay <whole> still, and because my brethren
George, Christopher, and the rest of my younger brothers were joint
executors to my late lord and father, whose soul I beseech Jesus Pardon.
My said two brethren promised to go thither at that time, for though
we never intended during [176v] my lord brother's life to make any
business for the same (yet if it should please God to call him to His
mercy, we would be glad to come by some part of my said lord and
father's money if we could by any lawful means after his time come
by the same), the rather, for that[67] we think my lady, my sister-in-law
[is] not the most kind to us.

At which time also Jones told me what fee he might have from the
abbot of St. Albans, but he said he would be with none of the fathers
of the cote but had rather be with some of worshipful blood and, upon
promise of reward, if the same journey took like effect, promised to go
my brothers George and Christopher contented likewise.[68]

Item after that, so riding, he told me that this realm should be
long without a king and much robbery would be within the realm,
especially of abbeys and religious houses and rich men as merchants
and grazers[69] and others. So if I would, he at the time would advise
me to find the means to enter the said castle for my own safeguard
and that diverse persons of their own minds would resort to me with
their goods for safeguard. To this I answered that there is nothing that
the will of God is that a man shall obtain but that he of his goodness
will put in his mind the means whereby he shall come by it and that
surely I had no mind to follow any such fashion,[70] and that the late

67. = but on the contrary, because
68. I.e., he preferred to work for
nobility rather than clerics, and if they
promised to pay him, was contented to
work for William and/or his brothers. There is a nota mark beside this
paragraph.

69. *grasyers*, i.e, those who graze
cattle.

70. The meaning of this passage is
muddy, but the implication is clearly that
Neville claims to have put his faith in the
will of God in these matters and would
not take matters into his own hands.

Duke of Buckingham, young Rise, and others had cast themselves away by means of too much trust in prophesies and other gambles of themselves. Therefore, I would in no wise follow any such way. Whereunto he said that if I would not, it would be long before[71] I obtained it. Then I said I believed that well, and if it never came, I trusted to God to live well enough. Then he talked anew[72] of the going northwards as is above, etc.[73]

Item I talked to him one time of one Agrippa that had made a book, late imprinted, *On Occult Philosophy*, which he said was of very small effect. Then I told him that some, as I have heard say, had the craft to make or draw the fashion of a bird upon a wall and by pricking of the same to destroy a bird upon a house, which methought was not likely.[74] He said that it might be done, but he said, he that used [177r] it should be suspect otherwise, saying that in the days of the King that is dead[75] (the King's Grace's most noble progenitor) two masters of art were sore punished for keeping of such images.[76]

Item he told me that none of Cadwaladre's blood should reign longer than twenty-four years.[77]

Item he told me that Prince Edward had a son which was conveyed over sea and there had issue, a son who is yet alive either in Saxony or Almagne, which I told him this was not likely, seeing that he had not been heard of in all this time. He said also that either he or the King of Scots should reign next after the King's Grace that now is.

Item he told me at Warwick in the morning while we lay there that he had fought three battles for me. First, he said a learned man came to him before the castle and asked him what he did there and after a few words he departed and after that another man who did likewise. At last in the middle of the town in the presence of diverse [people], one came to him and brought two white rods and offered to

71. *or*
72. *of new*
73. This paragraph has nota mark next to it.
74. Although the source is not clear, this idea was evidently in circulation in England. Reginald Scot describes the same magical process many years later in *The Discoverie of Witchcraft*

(London: W. Brome 1584), book 13, chapter 13, p. 308.
75. *dead is*
76. This paragraph and the following two have nota marks next to them.
77. On Henry VII, Arthur redivivus, and Cadwaller, see Coote, *Prophecy and Public Affairs*, 237.

try[78] with them. He said nay, he would try with the sword, and so did hit his adversary's sword, as he said, so nigh the hilt that the blade flew into the air, which done he departed. Then, he said, he returned into the castle. There in the afore named tower, he found a book binder[79] with three globes to be sold and the price as he said was an angel[80] a piece. So, we took up the same and departed. This he reported.

Item my brother George and Jones departed to Oxford again promising to come again before All Hallows' to go northwards. At which time Jones told me diverse things concerning my own business that proved not true, whereby I sustained loss [177v].

Item after that my brother Christopher and Thomas Wood, because he was desirous to go with me to Southcerney in Gloucestershire where I have a little land for term of life of my lord my father's gift (whose soul Jesus of his great mercy absolve[81]), where I intended to keep a court.[82] Lodged at Nash's house over night at Cirencester, being ten miles from the town of Southcerney, Nash told me that there should be three battles in those parts between the three masses. One at Hynam cross, beside Gloucester, another on the Seven Downs where the greatest lords belonging to it should be slain, of which he named the Duke of Suffolk to be one, and the third battle at a town beside Abyngton, the name whereof I do not remember.[83]

Item he told me that I should be Earl of Warwick within few years by the King's Grace's promotion. I told him others were nearer the possibility thereof than I—even[84] if it were so that I were Lord Latymer—if the King's grace were minded to give it to him that were next heir in blood. He asked me who and I said my Lord Montague. He said I should not need to care for that, for his eye should be out before[85] that time.

Item in that journey, I told Thomas Wood what Jones had said to me concerning Warwick and he said that, if it were such a troublesome world, he would have his part among them. Particularly of the abbot of

78. = battle
79. *boke byndre*. A book maker?
80. A gold coin worth seven shillings, six pence.
81. *assoyle*

82. A kind of cart. Poss. also literally court.
83. This paragraph is annotated "Nota. For to examyn Nashe."
84. *and*
85. *or*

Pershere and the parson of Fladbury, he advised me if any such time came that I should send to them to borrow some money from them.[86]

Item after that same Thomas Wood said to me in my gallery at Wick, "If you were Earl of Warwick it were good you had substantial officers and counselors." He desired himself to have the governance of the buckhounds and the rule of some park. Whereto I made no[87] answer, but I said if it pleased God and the King's Grace so to make me, I would be glad to have some sad and discrete gentlemen in fee as counselors if they would take the pain of which I named Master Winter to be one. Howbeit I doubted if I were so, whether he would be contented to be of counsel with me or no, because he hath fair lands of his own.

Item I remember that in the entering of the tower before named at Warwick, the keeper (as he commonly does to others in hope of reward) delivered me Guy of Warwick's sword to feel the balance[88] thereof and after Jones said you may see this as a token etc. [178r].

Item the said Wood brought me twice prophecies, whereof one was in parchment old written, another in his brother's hand. He told me that one Hurlock told the very time of the Scottish field and how that the King of Scots should be slain at it, which he said he was told before the field.

Item he offered me his service about a month before Christmas or thereabouts. Because I had enough servants and he was in debt as well for his rent as otherwise, I caused my wife make him answer that I would speak with him therein when he and I were even, for he had perfidiously done me diverse trespasses for which I was never recompensed.

Item whether the said Thomas Wood did ask me whether th<at I> could not make my lord brother out of the way <. . .> I remember not perfectly, but if he did, this was my answer: that <I would> never be about that while I lived.

Item upon All Hallows' Eve, Jones came to me with my brother and then told me that we need not greatly hasten northwards until about a seven night hence.

---

86. This paragraph has a nota mark next to it.

87. *none*

88. *payse*

Item on the morrow he desired to have one of my servants to ride with him in to Wales to his father's. He said he would bring a bruiter[89] with Welsh pedigrees and prophesies with him, which he did not, but came again himself.

Item Jones said that when he came out of Wales, the King's Grace had written a letter after the death of young Rise[90] that Wales should be destroyed, which I told him I believed not.

Item the said Jones gave me a ring of gold with the scripture of the double dictate[91] upon it, bearing me in hand that it was such a ring as he spoke of (but I perceived by one of his books the contrary) at the delivery whereof he said this: "God send you as much joy of it as ever had King Solomon that was the first deviser of these rings."

Item my brother George told me that Jones said to him that if the King's Grace came home, his highness should be driven <out> again by his commons, which I think was but to excuse <the> untrue reports that he had made before, for every man <ought to> know it was no likely thing.[92]

Item one William Wade told me that the King's Grace should speed very well beyond the sea but his highness should not marry before his grace return again [178v].

Item Wade said that he thought that the French king would not meet with the King's Grace beyond the sea but send, which was not true.

Item Wade told that there would be no field this year that is passed.

Item Wade told me that about certain years hence I should come to such marriage and other promotions, some by the King's Grace, and some by course of inheritance, as the others said. Nevertheless, I have found all their reports concerning myself untrue in other particular matters.

Item on the morrow after that Jones came to me from Wales, I asked him when we should go northwards and he said the field would be about a seven night before Christmas. Therefore, my brother

89. Generally, the term refers to one who spreads rumors.
90. *Rhys ap Gruffydd*

91. *dicate*—i.e., "double commandment" (Mark 12:29–31)
92. This paragraph has a nota mark next to it.

George and he promised to come again at St. Andrew's Tide, which they did not.

Item he would that I should have lent my brother George and him horses to go northwards before me, which I would not. I perceived that his intent was to have had a book, which he said a certain Friar Bacon had and was now in the church roof of the monastery of Dures<. . .>.

Item I came upwards by Oxford, sent for my brother George to my inn, with whom Jones came. I told him that his letter and other [of] his words was like to bring me in displeasure. Then he desired that he might alter the letter and I to have colored the matter, which I would not, but told him I would declare the truth.

Item diverse other communications of small effect I had with the said light persons, which I cannot at this time call to my remembrance, but I have touched the effect of all as nigh as I can. But so God help me, if I should die this hour, I would take it on my death that I never intended, neither by art of magic nor otherwise, to the hurt of the King's Grace's most noble person, nor never wished worse to his Highness than I would wish to my own soul. But by means of idleness and lack of sad company and virtuous exercise, I fell to fantastical imagination and curious desire to have knowledge of things to come, which is above the reach of any living creature but where almighty God of his special grace will give it. Greatly discomforted in my heart and shall be while I live that I had not the grace to perceive it till now (most chiefly of all that I have so highly displeased the King's Highness when I have found [him] at all times so good and gracious lord unto me) in the most humble wise that I can imagine, submitting myself to his grace and mercy without hope whereof I suppose verily I had not been alive in this house.

[unsigned]

1.4. Deposition of George Neville[93]

These are answers of Richard Jones[94] as concerning my brother William's fortune, the which he desired to know of, as far as I know by them both.

First, as concerning the Earldom of Warwick, Jones said that he should make my brother William in such favor with the King's Highness, that he should not desire that thing [the earldom] of his grace lightly, but he should obtain it and this he would bring to pass by his science. He wrote a letter to my brother in which he fiddled[95] that he should be Earl [of] Warwick for he named him so by [his] shield[96] <. . .>.[97]

Item he told my brother William, as my brother showed me, that he asked questions of my brother of a spirit which led him up into a tower. [Jones] told him of the manner of the tower and that Jones led my brother up to the highest chamber in the tower and that my brother was costly arrayed and that he had gear upon him after the manner of the creation of an earl, as my brother William perceived by his saying. For to have more perfect knowledge, the said Jones desired to go to Warwick to see if there were any such tower as he had seen in his visions. So by the reason thereof, my brother went and Jones and my brother Christopher and I rode thither at my brother William's desire. There he found in the tower that Guy's sword is in and when he saw it, he said it was the tower that he had seen.

Item Jones said to my brother that if there were war in the north parts and my lord my brother went thither, that he should be in great jeopardy and like to be killed. Therefore, I wrote a letter to my Lord that he should get license to tarry at Holund because it should not be good for him to go because it was told me so. So my brother William did, as I suppose.

Item that my brother should marry another wife by whom he should have more land than he hath by this [wife] within this two years.

---

93. TNA SP 1/72/179r
94. This is evidently a copying error as this is clearly George Neville.

95. I.e., told an entertaining story.
96. I.e., heraldic device.
97. Text undecipherable.

These are all that I know and can call to my remembrance, that Jones showed my brother that I know of. Therefore I humbly beseech your lordship and all you that be of the King's high and most honorable counsel to speak for me to his most Noble Grace to be gracious and merciful to me his poor subject, for as God knoweth—and so God me help at my most needy—I never intended no hurt nor prejudice to his most Noble Grace, nor was of counsel thereof at any time.

1.5. First Letter of Richard Jones to Cromwell[98]

Honorable lords, I take God to record that I did never commit nor reconcile treason since[99] I was born, nor imagined the destruction of no man or woman as God shall save my soul. He knows my heart for it is he that is *scrutator cordium*[100] and in him is all trust. I will not damn my soul for fear of worldly punishment, the joy of heaven [being] eternal and incomparable to the joy of this wretched world. Therefore, good lords, do by me as God shall. Put in minds, for[101] another day you shall suffer the judgment of God when you can not start from it,[102] no more than I can start from yours at this time. Now to certify you of all that I can.

William Neville did send for me to Oxford, that I should come and speak with him at Wick and to him I went. It was the first time that ever I saw him. I would I had been buried that day. When I came, he took [me] by [the] arm and went to his garden and there demanded of me many questions, and among all others asked were [it] not possible to have a ring made that should bring a man in favor with his prince, saying my Lord Cardinal had such a ring, that whatsoever he asked of the King's Grace, that he had.[103] "And Master Cromwell, when he and I were servants in my Lord Cardinals, did haunt to the company of one that was seen in your faculty.[104] Shortly after, no man [was] so great with my Lord Cardinal as Master Cromwell was. I have spoken

---

98. TNA SP 1/72/180r
99. *seth*
100. = the examiner of hearts
101. I.e., call to remembrance that . . .
102. I.e., escape it.
103. *that what some bere he askyd of the Kynges grace that he haddyd*
104. I.e., a cunning man.

with all them that have any name in this realm and they all[105] showed me that I should be great with my prince and this is the cause that I did send for you: to know what your saying be, agreeable to theirs or no" [180v]. I, at the hearty desire of him, showed him that I had read many books, especially the work of Solomon, and how his rings should be made and of what metals and what virtues they had after the canon of Solomon. Then he desired me instantly to take the pain to make him one of them, and I told him that I could make them but I made never none of them, nor I can not tell that they have such virtues or no, but by hearsay.

Also, he asked what other works had I read, and I told that I had read the magical work of Hermes, which many men doth prize, and thus departed at that time. One fortnight after, William Neville came to Oxford and said that he had one Wade at home at his house that did show him more than I did show him, for the said Wade did show him that he should be a great lord nigh to the parts that he dwells in, and in that lordship should be a fair castle. He could not imagine what it should be except it were the castle of Warwick. I answered and said to him that I dreamed that an angel took him and me by [the] hands and led us to a high tower and there delivered him a shield with sundry arms, which I cannot rehearse. This is all that ever I showed him, save [that] at his desire I went thither with him, and as concerning any other man, save at the[106] desire of Sir Gres, done night,[107] I made molds (that ye have) to the intent that he should have had mistress Elizabeth Gare [181r].[108] If any man or woman can say and prove by me otherwise than I have written, except I have at the desire of some of my friends called to stone for things stolen, let me dissent.[109] Touching Master William Neville, all the country knows more of his matter than I do, save that I wrote a false letter or two according to his false desire to make pastime, to laugh at. Also, concerning treasure trove I was oftentimes desired unto it by solicitous[110] fellows of the country, I never meddled with all. But to make the philosophers stone I will jeopard my life to do

---

105. *all they*
106. *they*
107. possibly "dun knight" for brown knight.

108. I.e., he otherwise only traveled with Neville and made magic images or rings for love for Sir Gres.
109. *disort*
110. *solyste*, possibly also "dirty."

it, if it please the King's Good Grace to command me to do it or any other nobleman under the King's Good Grace, and of surety to do it to be kept imprisoned till I have done it. I desire no long space, but twelve months upon silver and twelve and a half upon gold.[111] Which is better to the King's Grace than a thousand men de<...> for it is able to maintain a thousand men for ever more putting the King's Good Grace nor the realm to no cost nor charge. Also concerning our sovereign Lord the King's going over, this I said: if I had been worthy to be of his Grace's counsel, I would counsel his Grace not to [have] gone over that at that time of the year.

1.6. Second Letter of Richard Jones to Cromwell[112]

Right worshipful master, whose heart God has replenish[ed] with mercy and pity according to his saying: "*Hoc est preceptum meum ut diligatis inuicem sicut dilexi vos.*"[113] Also, James the apostle saith: "*Superexaltat misericordia iudicium. Iudicium enim sine misericordia erit illi; qui non facit misericordiam.*"[114] All this to you is well known, and for that that you have done for me I cannot recompense save I pray for you day and night as I am bound during my lifetime, for next [to] God and my prince ye have my heart. I would to God it were your pleasure to show to the kings good grace that I will be bound and my friends in 100 pounds or more to make the philosopher stone in twelve month and a half upon sol and twelve month upon lune.[115] For[116] if you were certain of it as I am, ye would pity that I lost so much time as I have lost hitherto, for it is a precious thing. For the Love of God almighty, [take] me to your service not as a servant but as one of your dogs and I trust to God to do your service in sundry things, which shall be to pleasure. This stone is to many men doubtful, for

111. *glod*
112. TNA SP 1/73/1r
113. = This is my commandment, that ye love one another, as I have loved you. John 15:12.
114. = Mercy triumphs over judgment. For judgment will be without mercy to anyone who has shown no mercy. James 2:13.
115. For dramatic effect, he uses the French words for sun and moon to mean gold and silver.
116. *For and*

many men have been deceived by [it] and not without a cause for they had not the knowledge of the right. *Nisi granum frumenti cadens in terra mortuum fuerit ipsum solum manet.*[117] Ask what suertes ye will, reasonably, and let me write to my friends and my friends shall bind themselves for me to the king's officers of the country, which you will, to Lord of Wysseter or else to Sir William Morgan, steward there as I was born, to perform my promise concerning the philosopher's stone. The love that I have to my prince compels me to do it, and not fear of imprisonment or death, for I never deserved in word, deed, nor thought, as God knows (in whom is all trust) that he has [and] does instruct your noble heart concerning me in all things. *Misereremini mei, misereremini mei.*[118] Your poor orator, Richard Johns.

[lv] Also, if it had please[119] your Mastership that I should have written a letter to Oxford, as master lieutenant promised, concerning Doctor London, ye had been certified before this of that. That would have made him smoke and other too of his affinity before this time.[120] If it will not please you that I shall write, let me be of a knowledge when ye send thither for ye shall have my mind for it must be handled[121] secretly for the most part of them be of one condition. Because I did talk of my lady marquess and you largely, they[122] did owe me a privy malice, which they durst not express that way, but imagined to bring me to my confusion by some other means. For they had taken great offense[123] that I should be among them and specially at my chamber, raiment, and books for they varied[124] before my face for my stuff. That Master Whitaker and Master Gethin can tell for they were there present. As concerning Master Neville, I would to God the King's good grace know him as well as the country knows him, for he made much pastime with his countenance in the country, but nothing that ever I heard concerning treason to the King's Noble Grace. For if I had heard, I would not have kept counsel no longer than I might have

117. = Unless a grain of wheat falls into the earth and dies, it remains just a single grain. John 12:23–24. Jones writes "interra" in place of "in terram."

118. = Have mercy upon me, have mercy upon me. The phrase invokes the *Agnus dei* from the Latin mass, which asks for God's mercy.

119. *plesue*
120. *other to of hys fynyte or this tyme*
121. *hondeles*
122. I.e., Doctor London and his associates.
123. *hoccore*
124. I.e., quarreled.

showed to one of the King's council. The most that I have offended was in laughing in his countenance as one would do at one of his behaving. Wherein I have offended my Lord God and I am punished *forte*[125] and I thank God of it as the trinity knows, to whom I pray for your good preservation.

1.7. Letter of Robert Webb to Cromwell[126]

Right Worshipful sir my duty done and according to my oath to my Master this is the cause of my writing, certifying you since my last being with you, which was at London, concerning the keep of the castle of Warwick. Since my coming home there is a priest of Guys Cliffe, which is of the foundation of the Warwick lands, that hath come to me upon his own mind and hath showed me that Neville, which is now in hold, hath been with him twice with certain priests with him and learned men desiring him to see pedigrees and chronicles where the said priest did copy him out a book, which book I have now in my custody. And the said priest did lend Neville another book, which book he hath still in his custody. Upon this confession, I have taken the book that the said priest did copy out into my own hands and the key of their library where all their books be, which every gentleman is desirous to see and that makes some of them to reign[127] in folly. For the priests be glad to show every gentleman pleasure. Also, I have made him write his own mind with his own hand desiring you to be so good, master, to me to advertise me what is the King's pleasure and yours: what ye will have done in this matter. For I have bound the priest to be forthcoming at all times at your pleasure. Therefore, desiring you send me your mind in this behalf, for it is not unknown unto you but late days that I was before you to my own costs and charges, beseeching you therefor to accept my mind and my rude terms of writing, for I send up my own servant on my own proper cost and charge, requiring you to be so good, master, to advertise me as shortly as ye can, thanking you ever for being so good to my brother and to me and we shall

125. Latin: strongly.
126. TNA SP 1/75/38r

127. *Reynge*

daily pray for you as knoweth God who ever preserve you. Written at Warwick the 21st day of March

By your beadsman Robert Webbe
Yeoman of the King's studs

1.8. Sir Edward Legh, Late Chaplain unto William Neville[128]

Beseeching your honorable lordships to have in remembrance the good and true service to my power done unto the King's Grace, putting myself in jeopardy against William Neville in his own house before all his servants and tenants to accuse[129] him face to face, before the constable and the whole town, charging them that he should not escape and called him traitor before them all, and he cast down his head and made no answer but went backwards into his chamber and no man durst lay hands on him. When I said that, I pressed towards him myself to have taken him, for there were three of his servants that took part with me for I told them before what he was. But he made fast the door that I could not come to him. Then his privy messenger John Lamb came to a poor man three times and William Neville himself commanded him to ask the peace on me and that while he made him ready to go his way and the constable was commanded to watch in the night and we to take heed in the day if he should come or go or move any goods until such time as we heard from the King's honorable Council. At the session when I should have discharged my sureties, the justice durst not discharge me, but made me to find surety to be ready to appear before the King's Council to justify my writing against William Neville. <Whereup>on I have lain five weeks and more at my cost and charge until the time <. . .>gs threatened[130] to fire the house where I lay then by the counsel [39v] of the justice of the shire seeing that all the parties went up to go before the King's Honourable Council. Because I was able to keep myself no longer for I had not my wages for he oweth me 16 s. 8 d. and I had never a penny of him (and for to make my costs to

128. TNA SP 1/75/39r This letter is to King's Council

129. *appetche*
130. *manysyd*

bring me up I have laid a gown to pledge for a noble, the which cost me five nobles, 3 s., 4 d. and if I pay not that within 14 days I shall lose my gown) wherefore I beseech your honorable lordships to let me have my wages to live upon because my money is gone. I will tarry at your commandments while it lasts, and if it please you to hear me speak before you, I shall show you the circumstance of his mind at that time with somewhat more behind because I had but short time the messenger made so great haste.

1.9. John Longland, Bishop of Lincoln, to the Duke of Norfolk[131]

My duty remembered unto your grace. Ascertain the same that on Saturday as I rode towards Woburn, I met with the commissary of Oxford, which showed me of two ungracious scholars called Jones and Neville and of the mysterious disposition of Jones. As he came towards London, he met with a man at Tattisworth called Roger, which asked for Jones. For as much as he did suspect the man to be conversant with the said Jones, he brought him to my house at Woburn and there left him that I might, at my coming, examine him. So have I done and his sayings I have, here enclosed, sent unto your grace that ye may perceive and know the same. [I] have also, herein enclosed, sent you a letter which he had sewed between the lining and the underside[132] of his coat. As yet I can get no further knowledge of him than is written. He is a simple person, and a poor body, and had two horses, one for Jones, another for himself, to have brought him to the said monk at Saint Albans. I shall keep him safe and his two horses till I know from you, either the King, his pleasure, or yours, what shall be done with him. Thus, the Holy Ghost preserve you in good long life with increase of much honor.

Written at Woburn the 12th day of January.
Your beadsman and priest, John Longland.

131. TNA SP 1/69/12. A short second letter from the Bishop to Cromwell asks again what he should do with Tyler [TNA SP 1/69/15]. John Longland was Bishop of Lincoln from 1521 to 1547.

132. *vttresyde*

CHAPTER 2

Power, Knowledge, and Influence

The Magic Texts

Richard Jones, the Oxford magician, had amassed an impressive collection of "diverse books," as well as equipment for conjuring and alchemy. The reports by others about the magic he performed allude to specific forms of necromantic magic commonly occurring in manuscript. This suggests that at least some of these books were actual necromantic handbooks. It is unclear how much magic he might actually have performed, but even if the books and equipment were merely props to him, he was clearly familiar with the written traditions of magic that we consider in this chapter. So, too, was William Neville, who, according to Edward Legh, owned a book containing magic "conceits," including one for invisibility.

The first text below (Text 2.1) derives from a collection of magic experiments the title of which identifies its contents as "consaytes," the same word as William Neville used for his book. It contains a variety of magic experiments for love, influence over superiors, sex, gambling, hunting, fishing, and other such conventionally masculine goals or fantasies. In short, it is just the sort of book William might have owned. The processes for achieving invisibility it contains are different from his but rely on similar notions about the occult powers in naturally occurring objects.[1] The same manuscript also offers another lurid operation for invisibility in which the magician conjures fairies who will bring him a ring of invisibility and will be willing to have sex with him.[2]

---

1. We know of no experiment for invisibility using shin bones, a buckskin, rosin, and glass.

2. Frank Klaassen and Katrina Bens, "Achieving Invisibility and Having Sex with Spirits: Six Operations from an English Magic Collection ca. 1600," *Opuscula: Short Texts of the Middle Ages and Renaissance* 3, no. 1 (2013): 1–14.

Magic manuscripts not only played to masculine fantasies or desires but also preyed upon masculine or patriarchal anxieties.[3] Men like William Neville, who were the head of a household, were ultimately responsible for preserving or enlarging their patrimony as a way of providing for their heirs and building social capital. These goals depended upon the unstable conditions of politics, personal favor, and patronage. As the dramatic rise and fall of many sixteenth-century courtiers illustrate—Cardinal Wolsey and Thomas Cromwell among them—one's fortunes could turn quite suddenly and unexpectedly. The concern to curry, maintain, or repair relationships with the powerful was thus constant. Letters we have already seen make this clear, particular those of William Neville and Richard Jones, whose lives literally rested in Cromwell's hands.

Unsurprisingly, magic texts also responded to the anxieties such conditions prompted. Texts 2.2 to 2.4 are only a small sampling of such operations and illustrate how the ring that Richard Jones offered to William Neville belonged to a very common sort of magic—one in which magical power inhered in an object. Engraved stones such as those found in Sahl ibn Bishr's *De sculpturis lapidum* were clearly meant to be worn in brooches or rings. The stone for honor or glory was to be set in gold and engraved with an image of a finely attired man with a scepter in his right hand and a stool in his left.[4] The passage on the Ring of Jupiter (Text 2.2) belongs to the same tradition of astral magic that is characteristic of texts derived from Arabic sources, which invoke astrological influences through hierarchies of spiritual creatures, in this case planetary angels.[5]

---

3. Naturally, these need not only be about sex and power. The *Ars notoria*, for example, offered learning and spiritual gifts to a clerical and learned clientele. Klaassen, "Learning and Masculinity."

4. "Quando invenitur in lapide homo ornatus, et in dextera ejus sceptrum, et et in sinistra ejus scabellum, hic positus in auro promovet ad honores. . . ." Thetel, "De Imaginibus,"

in "*Cethel aut veterum Judaeorum Phisilogorum de Lapidibus Sententie*," in *Spicilegium Solesmense III*, ed. J. B. Pitra (Paris: Institutus Franciae, 1852), 337.

5. For another example, see the operation to gain honor from a monarch in Thabit ibn Qurra, "De Imaginibus," in *The Astronomical Works of Thabit b. Qurra*, ed. Francis J. Carmody (Berkeley: University of California Press, 1960), 188–90.

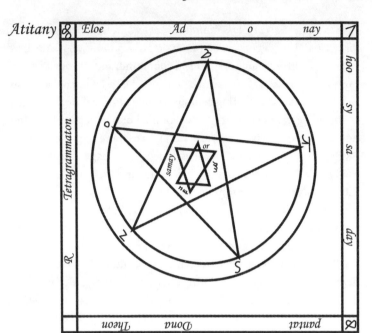

The image above, which has among its powers the ability to mollify the anger of magnates, appears in a seventeenth-century manuscript of the very rare *Four Rings of Solomon* and is also more representative of what William Neville might have expected in a magic ring.[6] Although it was in circulation, it seems unlikely that Jones used the *Four Rings of Solomon* given its rarity, the fact that the ring bears no relationship to the one Neville describes in his confession, and the fact that he does not actually claim to have had this text. Instead, Jones invokes Solomon's considerable reputation as a magician to impress his client.

Jones's ring of gold contained only "the scripture of the double dictate." This refers to Jesus's reduction of the law to two principles in Mark 12:29–31. This would be a lot to engrave on one ring but would be reducible to something like this: "*Diliges Dominum Deum tuum*

---

6. London, British Library, Sloane 3847, fols. 66v–81v. This ring appears on 67r.

ex toto corde tuo, et ex tota anima tua, et ex tota mente tua, et ex tota virtute tua. Diliges proximum tuum tamquam teipsum (Love the Lord your God with all your heart, and all your mind, and all your strength. Love your neighbor as yourself.)" Neville evidently knew enough about magic to suspect that a ring containing only liturgical fragments had probably been intended only as devotional or apotropaic. Nonetheless, Jones would have had reason to insist that the ring was credible. Its explicitly religious nature does reflect some aspects both of the Solomonic literature and also of necromantic literature in general. The operations for honor in the text *On the Uses of the Psalms* (Text 2.4), a work of Jewish origins that sometimes travels with necromantic works, involve little more than the recitation or writing of a psalm. In a similar vein, the short necromantic operation for influence (Text 2.3) employs an explicitly Christian prayer and includes saints' and divine names in its chalk conjuring circle. It was understood in all this literature that such invocations of scripture were inherently powerful.

Neville's description of Jones's rooms at Oxford confirms his [Jones's] familiarity with necromantic magic and also with alchemy. He claims to have seen alchemical equipment, a scepter and other things for conjuring the Four Kings, an image of white metal, a ball of crystal, and diverse books, putatively for the practice of magic. These objects, as well as his [Jones's] claim that he was guided by a spirit in his dreams, make clear that Jones not only represented himself as a necromancer but had (at least) acquired many of the tools associated with necromantic practice. The scepter, for example, appears as a ritual element in both Texts 2.1 and 2.3. Operations for the Four Kings are relatively common in late medieval necromantic texts. These demons were understood to rule over hosts of subservient demons, and the names and operations for conjuring them vary from text to text. The version below (Text 2.5) derives from a late fifteenth-century necromantic handbook. There is no record of Jones having employed a child scryer as does this text, but Jones certainly did have a crystal stone as this text requires. In some cases magicians did their own scrying. The Lord Cardinal's book with angels in it could also have been a magic book such as an *Ars notoria*, a work from the ritual magic tradition, or the *Sworn Book of Honorius* (*Liber iuratus Honorii*) a work including explicit conjuring. Versions of both of these works include illustrations of angels.[7] The final bit of evidence linking Jones to the necromantic tradition is his claim to have been offered the vision of Warwick Castle by a spirit. This accords with the sorts of texts we find in conjuring manuals.

The conjurations found in Texts 2.3 and 2.5 (particularly the sections written in English) require some additional commentary. Unlike most necromantic literature, they combine subservient and supplicatory language with outright commands and adjurations. The notion that magicians made implicit or explicit pacts with demons by worshipping or giving obeisance to them was a common criticism of necromantic magic. Unsurprisingly, the more typical posture in necromantic operations was one of domination, using the rhetoric of cursing and exorcism. Text 2.5 apologizes for its obsequious language by implying that this approach was a formality for dealing with angelic (if fallen) and kingly creatures. This kind of respectful treatment of demons of high rank appears to be more common in the sixteenth century and in vernacular manuscripts, but it is also clear that such an approach continued to be regarded as quite problematic even by fellow necromancers. A subsequent owner of the manuscript from which Text 2.5 is drawn crossed out the English prayers that took this approach and also tried to expunge the problematic phrases in the Latin prayers such as *supplico te* (I supplicate you), leaving the more imperious ones such as *coniuro te* (I conjure you) untouched.

In his description of Jones's rooms at Oxford, Neville also mentions books, seemingly magic books, owned by Cardinal Wolsey. This is curious, given that Jones elsewhere claims that Wolsey had a ring of influence. The cardinal's involvement in magic also seems to be corroborated in the William Stapleton case (discussed above) in which a demon reputedly said it was working for Wolsey. Later in the same account, the Duke of Norfolk is said to be concerned that Wolsey had set an evil spirit on him. As tempting as it might be, such evidence should not be taken as an indication that this very careful

7. See London, British Library, Royal 17.A.XLII (*Liber iuratus*) or Oxford, Bodleian Library, Bodley 951 (*Ars notoria*). For illustrations of the *Ars notoria*, see Michael Camille, "Visual Art in Two Manuscripts of the Ars Notoria," in *Conjuring Spirits: Texts and Traditions of Medieval Ritual Magic*, ed. Claire Fanger (Stroud: Sutton, 1998), 110–39.

courtier and churchman had engaged in magic. They seem more likely to have resulted from speculations (or grumbling) about his dizzying rise from obscurity to the halls of power, which could be accounted for by such claims. Jones also may have suggested that Wolsey had rings for inciting favor simply in order to convince Neville that he wanted one, too. His claim that these books belonged to the cardinal similarly may have been an attempt to claim close association with Wolsey and thereby increase his credibility.

Another element in the William Neville story bridges the line between magic and politics: the literature of prophecy. In significant measure, the literature of political prophecy in England was a form of thinly veiled commentary on the moral condition of the country. Much more than the literature of magic, prophecy was textually unstable and tended to continuously recycle elements to match changing political conditions. At the same time, it was associated with magic, particularly in the figure of the mythical wizard Merlin to whom a significant number of prophetic texts are attributed. The foggy line between magic and prophecy is also illustrated by the fact that Neville's cunning men discussed and sought out prophecies for him.

At the same time, relatively few prophecies or alchemical texts appear in the company of magic texts in late medieval manuscripts. This suggests that practitioners of magic, at least those who collected and wrote manuscripts of magic, were not simultaneously interested in these subjects. It might also say more about the nature of prophetic texts, which tended to have political rather than predictive purposes. That being said, Neville was not the only sixteenth-century person to seek information about the future through necromantic magic or to combine this with an interest in alchemy. Humphrey Gilbert clearly did both.[8] More significantly, through magical operations based upon late medieval scrying traditions, John Dee became convinced that he was *himself* a prophet.[9] He also practiced alchemy. It is thus possible that

8. Frank Klaassen, "Ritual Invocation and Early Modern Science: The Skrying Experiments of Humphrey Gilbert," in *Invoking Angels*, ed. Claire Fanger (University Park: Pennsylvania State University Press, 2011), 341–66.

9. Deborah E. Harkness, *John Dee's Conversations with Angels: Cabala, Alchemy, and the End of Nature* (Cambridge: Cambridge University Press, 1999).

Jones is an early example of an increasing fusion of magic, alchemy, and prophecy peculiar to the sixteenth century.[10]

Despite all the evidence, it remains unclear if Richard Jones *actually practiced* magic as he claimed. He may simply have been a con man. The evidence suggests he and Nash worked together in a calculating way as a team to string the nobleman along. The incident in which the old man welcomed William "to his own" also seems too fortuitous to have been anything but prearranged. At the same time, the two do not appear to have been very efficient at actually getting his money, which one might expect from professional con artists.[11] Jones also seems to have been convinced that he could successfully make gold, suggesting at least that he believed in his own abilities. So in the end, we cannot know for sure if he really performed magic and believed in it, mixed magic with invention, or concocted all of it for the sake of money.

THE TEXTS

2.1. To Go Invisible[12]

Go to a swallow's nest on Thursday morning when she have young ones and break all their legs and put out their eyes and bind their legs with virgin whole wire string and let them so remayn. Then the swallow will come and see them so tied together. She will fetch a stone that will make them see again and also loose their legs. Then upon the

10. Frank Klaassen, "Curious Companions: Spirit Conjuring and Alchemy in the Sixteenth Century," in *Knowing Demons, Knowing Spirits in the Early Modern Period*, ed. Michelle D. Brock, Richard Raiswell, and David Winter (London: Palgrave Macmillan, 2018), 145–70.

11. By comparison, see the manipulations of Gregory Wisdom in Alec Ryrie, *A Sorcerer's Tale: Faith and Fraud in Tudor England* (Oxford: Oxford University Press, 2008), 1–34.

12. London, British Library, Sloane 3850, fol. 145v. This volume contains a variety of magic texts in various hands of the sixteenth and seventeenth centuries. The section from which this passage is extracted (fols. 143r–166r), entitled "Of Loue, of Kardes, dies & Tables And other consaytes," was probably written around 1600 and contains a variety of short magical secrets or experiments.

next Thursday if thou seek, thou mayest have a stone in the nest. Take it out with thy right hand and thou mayest by it go invisible. Et fiat.

2.2. The Composition of the Sigil of Jupiter[13]

The sigil of Jupiter is to be graven in gold, silver, brass, or tin, in the day and hour of Jupiter, the Moon being in <. . .>[14] with trine or sextile aspect of Venus or Jupiter in a clear day and without thy house, without any coverture betwixt the sky and them, and a quiet air. It were good if Jupiter were in the ascendant or in his exaltation, and that the infortunes be removed according to the pretended purpose of the work. This is the form of the sigil of Jupiter.

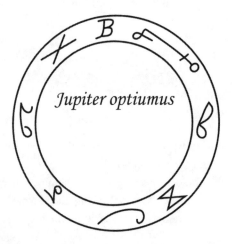

The form of this is many and marvelous in the operation of magic natural, the which in our time before few have known, for that the ancient wise men in the books that they have written, have very much hid their experiments.

13. Belenus, *De Sigillis Septem Planetarum* in London, British Library, Sloane 3846, fols. 45r–49r. Original in English. The manuscript includes a variety of texts of the early seventeenth century.

14. This is curiously left blank. Possibly the scribe was unsure about what was written in the source text.

THE COMPOSITION OF THE MASS WHICH MUST BE SIGILLATED

When thou wilt prepare the matter to sigillate with the sigil of Jupiter, which is most good and profitable, take the powder of the most white frankincense, cloves, saffron, red coral, [and] crystal stone called Cronioli of each a like quantity in weight and mix it with oil of roses or very good wine in the day and hour of Jupiter. Make thereof a mass like soft wax, whereof make many round pieces to the quantity of the sigil of Jupiter and let them be sigillated in either side.[15] Then let them be dried in the shadow, and put them in a secret place until you have occasion to use them. They have most excellent and marvelous effects.

While you are sigillating, say: "O Sadiell, most great angel of Jupiter excelling,[16] be thou present in this my doing, and let thy virtues be in this incense that I may accomplish and perform that [46r] which I desire, etc." and name that which thou desirest according to the petition to frame this occasion.

TO HEAL THE INFIRMITIES OF THE HEART

Give of this incense to drink to them that suffer grief of the heart and sides by reason of stopping of the blood or by any other occasion and he shall be healed thereof.

THAT LIGHTNING HURT NOT THY HOUSE OR BUILDINGS

Put seven sigils, whole not broken, with two great red corrals not having any holes through them upon the pinnacle of any tower in a vessel of tin or copper, and so long as it remaineth, there shall no lightning or tempest touch the building.

THAT NO WITCHCRAFT OR SORCERY BE DONE IN THY HOUSE

Take the substance of three sealings[17] and six grains of red coral having no holes. Wrap them together in a clean red cloth and bury it in the midst of thy house in the day and hour of Jupiter, and there may no witchcraft or sorcery be done in thy house.

15. I.e., press the carved sigil into the round pat of incense.

16. *precelling*

17. This either means three sigils or three lumps of the matter from which they are to be made.

THAT NO LIGHTNING OR TEMPEST HURT THY CORN OR FRUIT

Mix the powder of this sigil with powder of red coral, not holed, and with the seeds or sand, and so let it be sown about on the ground. There shall be no lightening or tempest hurt the fruits thereof forever [46v].

THAT THOU BE BELOVED OF ALL MEN

Perfume[18] thy garments and thy self so long or as oft as thou dost put on new apparel in the day and hour of Jupiter, and thou shalt be well accepted of, and beloved of, kings and prelates and judges. Whatsoever thou dost ask of them thou shalt obtain.

THAT THOU BE FORTUNATE IN ALL THY AFFAIRS

If thou dost bear this sigil upon thee, thou shalt be fortunate in all thy affairs and works and thou shalt prosper in honor, riches, and friendship with those that be of great calling.

THAT THERE BE PEACE AND CONCORD IN THAT PLACE WHERE IT IS DESIRED TO BE HAD

Sprinkle or sow about the powder of this sigil in any place or hour in the day and hour of Jupiter in which there is entreating for peace and concord, and there shall be peace with great joy.

TO HEAL ALL SUCH EVILS AS COME TO MAN OR WOMAN BY EVIL SPIRITS

If a man by means aforesaid or by witchcraft be touched in the night in sleeping so that there appeareth outwardly some redness, which happeneth oftentimes, take this sigill in powder and the earth alkaurt[19] and holy water. Make of them a plaster and put [it] on the place three days and it shall be healed most soon. But if it be in the body, wash his body with a bath tempered[20] with the aforesaid three things. So for three days space, wash the body well all [47r] over, beginning at the neck and so down to the feet. This must be done within seven or nine

---

18. The intent is evidently that the "sigillated" incense is to be used as a suffumigation for the operator and his clothing.

19. Poss. a form of alkali.
20. *balneam temperated*

days from the hour of the evil done unto the party justly accounted and not after.

TO CURE THOSE THAT ARE BEWITCHED SO THAT THEY CANNOT COPULATE[21]

If a man be bewitched so that he cannot copulate with his wife. Take[22] three sigils in powder in the washing of long pepper and the washing of the seed and the washing of cloves and beat all together into powder. Give it him for seven days space in the evening and in the night and in the hour of Jupiter he must begin to the weight of thirteen grains of barley in pottage made of peas, and that to use for his last drink. Let him use of that powder so much as he may suffer without danger, and if the aforesaid quantity be too little, double or treble the weight if need require, and so augmenting it until he be healed of that evil, which will be within nine days.

THE MARVELOUS EFFECTS OF THE SIGIL OF JUPITER IN A RING

If thou grave this sigil of Jupiter in a fair coral stone in the day and hour of Jupiter, he being in the ascendant or in his exaltation and the Moon being in Pisces or Sagittarius and Venus beholding Jupiter with trine or sextile. And let her be in Leo or if it may be, let Venus be with Jupiter. Put the stone so graven in his ring of gold, tin, or brass so that the graving of the stone do manifestly appear, and put [47v] under the stone a leaf of laurel in which must be written the names and characters of the ascendant and the lord of the ascendant of the nativity. I say unto thee that this ring hath many virtues and such marvelous effects that no man would believe except he had proved vt fecit author.[23]

HERE FOLLOW THE TOKENS AND VIRTUES OF THE SAID RING AND FIRST THAT THOU BE BELOVED

If this ring be made by thee, or most secretly by an other in thy presence, [and] if thou do wear it on the little finger of thy left hand, there shall be wrought marvels in thee. It cause thee to be beloved, and to

---

21. See Catherine Rider, *Magic and Impotence in the Middle Ages* (Oxford: Oxford University Press, 2006).

22. *Recipe*

23. = as the author has done

appear honorable as well unto men as unto women, so that they shall honor thee greatly, and with a most high laud, praise thee and thy counsel, and shall perform thy sentences. Thy fame and name shall spread over the land. If thou wilt write after the faculty and science of writing and doctrine, it shall marvelously augment thy wit and memory, and it doth make the bearer of it sapient and eloquent above all other of his calling and all shall marvel at thee. It profiteth against all witchcraft so that in no case it can hurt thee. It withholdeth blood from what place so ever it doth come. It putteth back and taketh away all agues and griefs [48r] of the stomach and head. It obstructs[24] the hurt of lightning and maketh the bearer fortunate. It maketh most quickly peace and concord betwixt them that be in discord. The virtues of this ring be infinite, so that no man knoweth thereof the secrets it profiteth in all things as the sigil in powder doth.

2.3. An Experiment to Obtain Special Honor or Love of Whom Thou Wilt[25]

First you must have a fair, boarded chamber and to be clean from sin and with all your instruments belonging to this art. Then take chalk and chalk your circle in the hour of Venus and enter the circle in the same hour and turn ye to the south and say thus:

"I conjure you, Almazin and Elicona, most loving and gentle spirits by the infinite wisdom of God and by his great power and by the meekness and virginity of Saint Mary the Virgin, and by her chastity and cleanness, and by all the names of our Lord, Jesus Christ, and by that ineffable name of our Lord, the living God, Tetragramaton + which is graven in my scepter and in my ring,[26] and by the rending[27] of the

---

24. *letteth*

25. London, British Library, Sloane 3853, fols. 184–185. Original in English. A volume of conjuring texts containing material by two scribes (fols. 1r–174v and 175r–268r). The first is certainly sixteenth century, the second from which we have extracted fols. 184–185, perhaps as late as

the early decades of the seventeenth century.

26. This phrasing and the equipment used suggest the late medieval conjuring manual *Treasury of Spirits* (*Thesaurus spirituum*) inspired this operation.

27. *ryvynge*

wall of the temple,[28] and by the appearing of them that were dead and buried, and by the resurrection of the dead, through the death of our Lord Jesus Christ and by that most fearful day of judgment of Jesus Christ, that in as much as you can, you shall labor, and cause to labor, to set amity and love between N.[29] and N. without any feigning, fraud, dissimulation or crafty coloring of amity or love. The which precept and request of me if you shall neglect or despise and shall not do it for so much as you are able to do, that God condemn you with everlasting torments whose name you despise [184v] and condemn and violate his wisdom. Grant this, our Lord and yours, Jesus Christ, which in the trinity doth live and reign, God, world without end. Amen."

This done, do what you will, for you shall never see them, but they will fulfill it surely. Finis.[30]

28. Matt 27:51.

29. An abbreviation for *nomen* (name) standing in for the name the spirit being summoned.

30. = The end.

2.4. Psalms for Influence[31]

Say this psalm: "As a deer longs for flowing streams."[32] Also if you should be in danger and should come before the law or a judge or a lesser one, write this psalm and tie it on your arm: "The unjust hath said."[33]

To please the judge and to have him merciful, read this psalm before you come before him: "In thee, O Lord, I have hoped"+.[34]

If thou dost desire to have the love of any worshipful man, write his name and his mother's name & bend it under thy right arm hole and bear it with thee and thou shalt have his love.

If thou wilt have what thou rightfully desire or ask of any worthy man, write this in parchment and hang it on thy right arm and read it often times and thou shalt have thy desire: "God, make firm my justice."[35]

Who desireth rightfully any thing of God let him say this psalm devotedly before the altar: "How long, Lord, will you forget me?" and "To you I lift up my eyes."[36]

He that desireth any thing of God let him say three times "to thee I have lifted up my soul."[37]

2.5. For the Four Kings in a Crystal or Mirror[38]

Say this prayer once with a good mind, then say the other one following for the boy and for your salvation and in supplication and conjuration

31. Cambridge Additional 3544, p. 85. This passage, in a mixture Latin and English, is drawn from a sixteenth-century conjuring manual in a single hand. The whole text is available in Francis Young, *The Cambridge Book of Magic: A Tudor Necromancer's Manual* (Ely, UK: Francis Young, 2015).
32. Ps 41 (Vulg.)
33. Ps 35 (Vulg.)
34. Ps 30:2 (Vulg.)
35. *deus iudicium meum regida*, probably a mistranscription of Ps 71

(Vulg.). "*Deus iudicum tuum regi da* (Give the king your justice, O God . . .)"
36. Pss 12 (Vulg.) and 122 (Vulg.)
37. Ps 24 (Vulg.)
38. Oxford, Bodleian Library, Rawlinson D. 252, fols. 15r–23v. The text begins in Latin. This volume is a late fifteenth-century necromantic manual by two scribes including a variety of conjuring texts mostly in Latin and largely concerned with treasure hunting.

of the kings, humbly supplicating, asking, binding, constraining, and conjuring in this manner thus:

Over you and the boy: "In the name of the Father and Son and Holy spirit. Amen." Then this prayer. Repeat it four times in every operation.

"God, you who ascended the holy cross and illuminated the shadows of the world, grant me that every work of mine may begin through you, and that the things begun may also be concluded through you.[39] Omnipotent eternal God, you who have most noble and infinite power, most worthy dominion, and names wondrous in the whole earth, I pray you by your holy virginity, by your holy death, and by your holy dominion that no malign spirit should be able to resist these orders that I give in your name and in the name of all the saints, through our Lord Jesus Christ, your son, who lives and reigns with you God world without end. Amen" [fol. 15v].

The second prayer [begins] with "In the name of the Father and of the Son, etc." over you and over your boy.

"God of Abraham, God of Isaac, God of Jacob, God who formed Adam out of the earth in your own image, God who brought forth Eve from the side of Adam, God who discharged[40] Adam and Eve to sin in paradise, God who discharged Cain to kill Abel, God who came from the bosom of the Father for the redemption of the world, God whose will it was to be conceived of the Virgin Mary[41] and was born, God whose will it was to be captured by your enemies the Jews,[42] grant me and this boy to do well and speed well without harm either to my body or the boy's, and to my soul or the boy's, and grant that every spirit of the air that I invoke in this work, obey and serve and not contradict me and this boy, but let him have a pure vision in this glass or crystal stone for seeing those three kings, Oriens, Egyn, Paymon, and in this glass,

---

39. Similar to votive prayer "*Cuncta nostra operatio a te semper incipiat et per te cepta finiatur*" recorded by Christopher Wordsworth, *Ceremonies and Processions of the Cathedral Church of Salisbury* (Cambridge: University Press, 1901), 125.

40. *dimisisti*

41. *qui concipere voluisti de maria virgine*

42. *a iudeis inimicis tuis capere voluisti*

this king, Amaymon, without impediment to [16r] the boy's senses, or whatever spirits I invoke in this work through your greatest power and virtue and in accordance with which[43] O Lord Jesus Christ, you who are the salvation of the world, savior of the world, redemption of the world, we are not worthy of seeing your holy angels in this glass. I invoke you. I supplicate you diligently with all my mind that you deign to give us license to see your angels who serve from such offices through Christ our lord. Amen.

"Omnipotent, eternal God, you who are the way of truth,[44] whose will it was to be led by the false Jews before Pilate and accused by false witnesses. O Jesus the Nazarene, son of God, whose will it was to be taken and whipped by the hostile Jews and in the headquarters of King Caesar to be condemned and led to the Mount of Calvary and in the said place in the cross to be lifted up and crucified. Just so I ask you Father omnipotent, who are three and one and in the same manner by your virtue and power and by all your holy names, may all the spirits of the air be captured and led to us that [16v] those whom I invoke may in no way flee but, hearkening to me, benignly obey.

"O Lord Jesus Christ, King of Glory, whose will it was to be fixed on the cross with nails by Jews, thus let them be fixed by me, your servant, N., with your holy names so that they may be obedient, forbearing, and useful servants in all things, until I have my will fully completed[45] by them, and not more rebellious to me than you. O Lord, were to the Jews, your enemies. O Lord Father and God of all who then permitted, while Longinus the soldier [was] with him, for your side to be pierced with his lance, I beseech you, omnipotent Father, that you deign to send me permission by your sacred virtues and names, while speaking with those spirits, that their sides be pierced just as your side was pierced by the common lance, that they answer to me concerning whatever affair I ask them about and obey my precepts.

"O King of Kings and Lord of Lords who discharged blood and water to flow from your side to complete the holy prophecy of your

43. *ex quo* [read *ex qua*]. There may also be a line skip here resulting in missing text.

44. Text obscure, but this echo of John 14:6 seems most likely.

45. *pleniter perfenitam* [read *perfectam*]

holy [17r] prophets. I bless and praise you, merciful Christ, that you grant to me domination and power by your names that must be named[46] to fulfill my desire as your prophecy was fulfilled by grace. O Lord, you who are life, virtue, truths, and salvation who discharged yourself to be crucified surrounded by thieves and were given gall and vinegar to drink. Discharge, I beg of you eternal God, that all aerial spirits surrounded by your holy names spoken by me (although unworthy), be crucified by those holy [names], as if they were given gall and vinegar to drink by them if they do not completely fulfill my desire in all requests.

"O my Lord, Son of God, under whose head was written in Hebrew, Greek, and Latin *Iesus Nazarenus Rex Iudeorum*,[47] grant to me and this boy to do well [and] to go forward without injury, vexation, or damnation of either soul or body.

"O Lord Jesus Christ, full of infinite virtue, who destroyed our death by dying, and restored by rising again, omnipotent eternal Father, you who were in the tomb for two days and on [17v] the third day arose from the dead, just so from the seats and all places in the whole world, in latitude as in longitude, may the spirits rise up and come to me in most beautiful human form at my first, second, or after my third invocation visibly to the sight of this boy and to me in this glass with no hindrance in any way intervening with those who[48] come to me, whom I invoke in this work through these, your principal names: Agla. Tetragramaton. Alpha. et [Omega]. Ageos. Otheos. yskyros. Athanatos. panton. Craton. ysus. Saluator. panton. agla. et Aglatos eye assarhe.

"Omnipotent, eternal God who cast out seven demons from the body of Mary Magdalene, omnipotent eternal father who discharged your holy apostle Thomas to touch your wounds when he did not believe that you had been crucified, O Lord Jesus Christ crucified, who from Galilee [18r] ascended wondrously to heaven, and sits at the right

46. Text has *non nominandis* which seems to be a mistranscription of *nominis nominandis*.
47. The basis for the abbreviation INRI, meaning Jesus the Nazarene, King of the Jews.
48. *intercurrentem quem*, assuming *intercurrente qui* with finial macrons inserted in error.

hand of the father, and from there will come to judge the living and the dead, grant to me and this boy that he is able [to see] in this glass for the three kings, Oriens, Egyn, and Paymon, and in this glass King Amaymon, and without impediment of our sense and without harm in any way, these four kings, that is Oriens, Egyn, Paymon, and Amaymon, by your holy name, which is blessed world without end. Amen."

With the petitions finished in this way, begin to invoke one after the other until you have all four together either in glasses or stones, with this opening benediction over yourself and over the boy.

"In the name of the Father and of the Son and of the Holy Spirit. Amen. O King N., who has power over all spirits who are under your regality.[49] I ask you, I command you [18v], I invoke you, I adjure you, and I conjure you by these names of Christ, Father omnipotent, King of all Kings, and Lord of all Lords: Agla. Tetragramaton. Alpha. et [Omega] Ageos. Otheos. yskyros. Athanatos. Panton. Craton. Ysus. Saluator. Panton agla et Aglatos. That you appear[50] before this boy and me visibly in this glass, as I ask by your concession and supplicate from your gift and rule. I bind and constrain and conjure and firmly order by all the divine names and by your own proper power which you have over all spirits of the air under your standing rule [that] I should have my will fully completed in all respects according to my own proper petition. To this end I ask and conjure you by the nine names of Christ: Lay. Hely. Hely. Lamazabatany. Tetragramamay. Adonay. Adonay. Algramamay. Aberegney. And by these two names Yoth Nabaoth [19r] I supplicate you, I ask you, I order you, I constrain and conjure you wherever you may be by the nine names of the angels, that is Michael. Raphael. Gabriel. Daniel. Thobiel. Uriel. Barachiel. Cherubyn. et Seraphyn. And by the holy and most chaste mother of our Lord Jesus Christ and by her most worthy five joys which she had from her son our redeemer, that you immediately without a backward glance go into this glass and fully, without defect fulfill my intention in the name of the most high Father and [Holy] Spirit paraclete."

49. *sub tuo regalite in amisisio* [read *regalitate*]. The latter two words are not intelligible and have been omitted from the translation.

50. *comparas* [read *compareas*]

It is necessary for this invocation to be said three times and always by the third time each and every one of them will come in turn. You will have them in this way. You will greet them in speaking with these angelic beings[51] humbly in this way:[52]

"Reverend Lords, God save you, bless you, and keep you. I am greatly beholden to you for your hither coming and therefore I thank you with all my heart that ye will do so much in any thing that toucheth [19v] towards me whereby[53] the lords the which are principals over all other spirits reigning under your regality in all the parts of the air would deign[54] of your high power and your own great goodness to come so soon to me at my calling you, praying in all manners (beseeching as falleth to a Christian man to do to lords of the air and principals, most worthiest of all other spirits) through the virtue and the powers of God, my former and yours, whose[55] virtue and power is above all virtues and powers, or[56] else by your own great virtue and your high power that ye lords haveth above all other spirits worthy and unworthy, great and small, that ye will of your highness, that your great, royal power deign,[57] and to me only, grant, for to be humble and obedient, as it falleth for lords royal [20r] for to be gracious, the time that I shall live and with you I cast me only to work,[58] and that you be obedient or humble to no man[59] in any manner degree, being in any country under the sun, having wit or wisdom or any manner [of] intelligence touching towards mankind but only to me or else to any of my deputies[60] of my own proper will."

But if it happens that they are rebellious and unwilling to obey the precepts and to appear at the aforesaid invocation, then begin with this following invocation.

"O King N., I supplicate you, I ask you by the true God, one and holy who is alpha et omega, and I invoke you by the power of our

---

51. *in angelicis loquendo illis*

52. The next paragraph is written in English.

53. *where that*

54. *yat wolde witsafe*

55. the which

56. *and*

57. *wytsaffe*

58. It seems likely that the intent is "during the time that I commit myself to work solely with you" rather than some promise of exclusively working with these spirits.

59. *ye obedient nor humble you to no man*

60. *assignes*

Lord Jesus Christ, who for the salvation of humankind, descended from heaven, was born of the Virgin Mary, and by the holy paraclete and *saeculum per ignum*.[61] I adjure you, N., by the holy paraclete, who proceding from the father and the son in the form [20v] of a dove rested over Christ in the Jordan river and over the apostles speaking in various tongues of the great deeds of God.[62] I ask you by the three persons in the Trinity, and I constrain by their virtues and powers. I invoke and conjure you by the unknown things of the angels and archangels. I adjure you by the Father and the Son and the Holy Spirit, and I constrain by the virtue of the undivided Trinity and by the lamb sitting in the throne of God and by the seven horns, which God ordained to be the seven sacraments. I conjure you by the Thrones and Dominations, Principalities, Cherubym, and Seraphym, and all the powers of heaven. I invoke you by their armies and constrain by those who unceasingly proclaim[63] in an eternal voice, "Holy, holy, holy." I ask and conjure you by the forty elders, carrying their bowls in hand, and falling prostrate before God and by their white crowns and assiduities.[64] I supplicate by the twenty-four martyrs [21r] and I adjure by thunder, flashes, and lightening of God. I conjure by the seven golden candelabras and the brightness when they stand before God with their lights. I ask and conjure you by the gold censer[65] in the hands of the holy angels of God, who made the odor. I supplicate you by the patriarchs and prophets, and I constrain you, by all the saints, apostles, and four evangelists, and by the fellowship of holy martyrs who suffered through the love of God. I ask you and conjure you by all the masses that are sung or celebrated through the whole world, and by the nine learned presbyters and by the nine boys newly baptized and by the nine altars of God. I supplicate by the annunciation of Christ, by the nativity of Christ. I ask you by the circumcision of Christ. I invoke you by the baptism

---

61. Lit., and the world by fire. This is an abbreviation of the standard liturgical phrase *qui venturus est iudicare vivos et mortuos,et saeculum per ignem* (who will come to judge the living and the dead and the world by fire).

62. For dove, Matthew 3:16, Mark 1:10, Luke 3:22, John 1:32. For Pentecost, Acts 2:11.

63. for *proclamancia* read *proclamant*

64. sinalas suas perortantes [read *fialas suas portantes*] The passage seems to allude to Rev 4:4–10 and 5:5–8.

65. Rev. 8:3; Heb. 9:4

of Christ. I adjure you by the fasting of Christ. I constrain you by the transfiguration of Christ. I conjure you by the mountain and passion [21v] of Christ. I bind you by the crown of thorns which the Jews put on the head of Jesus Christ and the reed and his right hand bearing it—and they knelt before him when they were mocking him and said, "Hail, King of the Jews"—and by the blows the Jews gave him, looking down[66] on him, and by the cross on which the Lord was hung, and by the cry of the Son to the Father saying, "Heloy. Heloy. Lamazabatam," and by the death of Christ by the lance by which Christ's side was pierced,[67] by the whips of Christ, by the nails with which the body of Christ had been nailed, by the wounds of Christ, and by the bread which God took, blessed, broke, and gave to his disciples saying, "This the chalice of my blood of the new covenant," which for us and many others was poured out in remission of sins, by the linen in which the Lord was wound,[68][22r] and by the sepulcher in which he was buried, by Christ's descent into Hell and his coming on the third day, and by the collective great works and wonders of God, that wherever you are, you now appear and enter into this mirror or glass visibly to the sight of this boy N. and me in beautiful human form having a king's beautiful red or white color, crowned with a golden crown, and give a true response to us, according to ability concerning whatever I ask you, by speaking to this boy and to me without injury to us and without impediment to the boy's senses or mine or any other deceit, and without harm to us or any other creature under the power of the majesty of God, neither to body nor to soul."

Then the master should ask the boy what he sees, and if he says, "I see nothing," then he [the Master] will call again twice or a thrice until they appear. When [22v] you have them all together, adjure them in this way:

"By all the things that I have said and conjured, I conjure you that you do not leave these glasses or this glass until you are permitted by me."

---

66. *aspicientes* [read *despicientes*]
67. *lanceam qua latus christi fuit perforata* [read *perforatum*]

68. *per lintheum in quo volutum* [read *volutus*] *erat dominus*

Then ask whatever you desire, and it will be given to you if you perform well, since most beautiful is the art of spirits, because in no other way will you be able to bind them and in this way you will bind them fully. Moreover, they will appear by invocation. And when you have had [your] desire fulfilled, you will license them in this manner:

"By all the things that I have already said and conjured and by all the things that have been done under the power of the majesty of God, I bind you all at the same time and your entire bodies, from the top to the bottom of your feet, with no part of your body left out, that you be always obedient to me with all things being discharged, however and wherever, in whatever place, inside or out, that I invoke you, all at the same time, one, two, or three without any impediment so long as I want, that you fulfill my desire in all respects without [23r] lies or guile, without jeering or fraud, and without terror or any deceit and without harm either of body or of soul, and that no one from the natural form of human kind in the world should you serve when I have something to do with you except me alone, unless you receive a license[69] from me or an operator licensed by me, and that at my opening of this book and by [my] invocation, you will always come together at once, without a backward glance, from any part of the world wherever you may be, and show yourselves to my presence, and also that you render up your very selves as servants making things ready, with these holy names[70] constraining you, in all hours of the day or night insofar as you are able: Adonay. Sabaoth. Adonay. Cados. Adonay. Annora. Thus I license you [to depart] at present until another time when I will invoke you."

Then he [the Master] should sign himself and the boy on the forehead with the sign of the holy cross thus, "In the name of the Father, and Son, and Holy Spirit." These things having been done thus, let him say, "May the peace of Christ be between us and you," and say, "In the beginning . . ." the whole gospel[71] and in the end, "Christ conquers, Christ reigns, Christ defends his servants from all evil. Amen. [23v] In the name of the Father and of the Son and of the Holy Spirit. Amen."

69. *licencia* read *licenciam*
70. *in omnibus* [read *nominibus*] *sacris*

71. Presumably, the intent is to read the prologue to the Gospel of John, which would be conventional, rather than the entire gospel.

And let him go out wherever he wishes.

And give them the proportions of the suffumigations in this way for a pleasant odor so that they might be pleasant to you. Take one ounce of powdered laurel leaves, one ounce of powdered balsam leaves, 1 pennyworth of pure balsam and let [someone] throw them in a fire of aloe wood, saying, "Take in the pleasant aspects of the odor."[72]

And whenever you want to operate through the kings, do so in this way.

---

72. *Accipe in suauis odoris.*

PART 2

Magic and Ecclesiastical Authorities

CHAPTER 3

The Fellowship of the Mixindale Hoard

The Legal Documents

The old West Riding of Yorkshire was the isolated, wild end of an isolated and independently minded area: the perfect place to conjure for treasure, or so it would seem. Most West Riding villages were small, and everyone knew everyone else's business. The nine men who gathered in the village of Bingley on January 28, 1510, to secretly conjure for the Mixindale treasure had undoubtedly aroused curiosity. Although they were cautious, they were clearly not cautious enough. It was not long before the news of their activities had spread all the way back to York.

The Mixindale case is preserved in an incomplete set of records copied into Archbishop Bainbridge's register. These reveal a complicated story that unfolded over the space of about twelve months before the participants were caught, but the sequence of events can be difficult to discern. The archbishop's officials were centrally concerned not with the temporal order of events but rather with the participants' heretical beliefs and public rumors about them. Also, the ten men (nine treasure hunters plus one witness) who were examined were frequently unclear and sometimes either accidentally or purposefully misleading. Each one tells a slightly different version of the story.

SUMMARY OF THE PARTICIPANTS AND EVENTS

The Mixindale treasure hunt of 1509 appears to have been promoted initially by William Wilson, servant to Ottwel at Hagh of Bingley. Wilson had been inspired to this endeavor by stories that a local man named Robert Leventhorp reputedly had seen a chest through a hole

TABLE 2: List of People Involved in the Mixindale Treasure Hunting Case

Members of the Mixindale Fellowship

Greenwood, Sir[1] Richard	Priest of Bingley
Hagh, Ottwell at, of Bingley	Resident of Bingley (50 years old)
Jameson, Thomas	Merchant of York, Sheriff in 1497 and Lord Mayor in 1501[2]
Knowles, Lawrence, of Harrogate	A servant of John Steward (38 years old)
Richardson, Sir James	Priest of York
Steward, John, of Knaresborough	Cunning man and former grammar school teacher
Wilkinson, Sir John	Austin Canon of Drax Abbey and priest of Bingley[3]
Wilson, William (aka William Ottwell)	Servant of Ottwell at Hagh (21 years old)
Wood, Thomas	Servant of Sir Richard Greenwood (35 years old)

Other people mentioned in the documents

Bank, Sir Henry	Chaplain of Addingham, witness
Brother of Richard Greenwood	No name given; resident of Bingley
Greenwood, Edmund (alias Michel of Heptonstall)	Richard Greenwood's father; resident of Bingley
Halywell	A monk from Salley who, together with Leventhorp and Watson, had seen the treasure before
Leventhorp, Robert, of Bradford	Had seen the treasure before in the company of Watson and Halywell
Watson of Wakefield	Had seen the treasure before in the company of Leventhorp and Halywell

1. Sir = Father. The title Sir (Dominus) was frequently used for parsons prior to the Reformation.
2. Victoria County History, York 3:206.
3. Victoria County History, York 3:205–8. The Priory of Drax held the parish church of Bingley.

in the ground but claimed that when he poked at it with his sword, the devil broke the blade off and pulled the treasure underground.

Sometime before Michaelmas (September 29, 1509), Wilson claimed to have convinced two priests at Bingley, John Wilkinson (aka the Canon of Drax) and Richard Greenwood, to go treasure hunting. Greenwood's servant Thomas Wood was included in the scheme at some point as well. They must have decided early on to conduct the hunt using necromantic magic, because when Wilson told his master Ottwell at Hagh about their plan, Wilkinson had to reassure Ottwell that the practice was not sinful. Encouraged by the priest, Ottwell admitted that he too became a treasure hunter. Greenwood and Wilkinson knew where help could be found; in the course of their examination, both of them admitted to sending letters to John Steward, a known magic practitioner and cunning man, who lived some ways north in Knaresborough. In his examination, the cunning man Steward claims this communication began about a year before the trial, roughly around May of 1509, which, if true, was quite a bit earlier than William Wilson's "before Michaelmas."

John Steward, like the priests of Bingley (Wilkinson and Greenwood), had connections. Steward drew into the treasure-hunting scheme James Richardson (a priest from York) and Thomas Jameson (merchant and ex-mayor of York), both of whom he had clearly worked with before. Richardson admitted to having known Steward "for some time" prior to these events. When Jameson's servant had run off with some of his possessions, Richardson suggested that the cunning man Steward could help locate the thief by means of magic. Richardson and Jameson rode to Knaresborough for this purpose. The operation evidently did not succeed, as they were still looking for the servant in the following year in March 1510.

Precisely when Steward invited the priest and former mayor to join the treasure-hunting project remains unclear, but Lawrence Knowles (Steward's servant) testified to having brought a gift of a shoulder of venison and a capon to Richardson from Stewart at Christmas 1509. Steward was evidently encouraging both Richardson and Jameson to get involved, although both claim this did not happen until January 6, 1510. Certainly by that time all nine men were involved.

Perhaps prior to Christmas 1509, but undoubtedly afterward, Wilkinson and Steward shared their books of magic (i.e., books of "experiments" or "experience") with the others. Richardson made copies of these books and also three conjuring circles from virgin parchment that had been given to him by Steward. Assuming they needed other equipment, such as the scepter and crown mentioned in the examination and perhaps a ring as well, they would also have had to make these, which would have taken some time.

All the collected evidence agrees that the nine men met at the house of Ottwell at Hagh in Bingley to make their attempt on the treasure on Monday, January 28, 1510. A good deal of preparation remained to be done. Thomas Wood said the priests performed two masses and later in the day he made confession to his master Richard Greenwood to protect himself from the demons. It is likely that all the men heard mass and confession in a similar manner, something that is typically required in necromantic handbooks. Steward took responsibility to gild the scepter—that is, to apply gold leaf to it. The priests, who had arrived with a large bag of equipment, probably including a magic crown and certainly a portable altar and holy water strinkle, hurriedly copied consecrations from a mass book for their operations. When all was prepared, they decided to leave the house in small groups so as not to arouse suspicions in the town. They would all meet some miles to the south on the moor at Solen End (most likely modern Soil Hill) at sunset.

The night was a complete debacle. Only Thomas Wood and his master Richard Greenwood made it to the rendezvous point. As both were from the area, and Richard seems to have been regarded as the guide, this makes sense. Although Solen End is a high point of land and easily visible under normal circumstances, a "great mist" came up. This would have accelerated the coming of darkness and blocked any moon or even starlight. As a result, the others spent the night wandering around on the moor at Bradford Dale Head. First, they ended up at a small town called Cockham, where they got fire for their torches (and seemingly salt to make holy water). They then wandered around looking for "the cross," where they seem to have thought the treasure was located. They went to a cross at Micklemoss (the wrong one) and paid a local to help them find the other, but to no avail. Not only was the night an uncomfortable and frustrating failure, but Richardson also lost the holy water strinkle on the moor.

Eventually, Wilson and Knowles were sent to get horses and bring them back to Cockham for Steward, Wilkinson, and Jameson. By this point another plan was being hatched. They would meet in Arden Wood, near Bingley, and Wilkinson would have the treasure brought to them by the spirit Belphares. But this also went awry. For some reason Wilkinson did not make the rendezvous, possibly because Richard Greenwood did not give him clear information, but also possibly because he had begun to worry that too many people now had an inkling of what was going on. In fact, Greenwood complicated things by bringing an additional two people into the conspiracy, his brother and father. The affair at Bingley dissolved into bickering over what to do next, what to do with the parchment circles, and how they would divide the treasure. Knowles cryptically said that the priests wanted to "set a little thing" at Gilside, possibly another magic operation, and that Jameson prevented it. This may explain why they angered Jameson by mocking him for his lack of learning. One way or another it was the end of the Mixindale fellowship. The party finally fully dissolved on Thursday, the last day of January in 1510.

Even before they had all left Bingley, however, a smaller group had reaffirmed their resolve to get the treasure. This included the priests Greenwood and Wilkinson, and also the former mayor Jameson, who evidently had resolved his differences with them, but they excluded John Steward, the cunning man. They continued to work, focusing their efforts in York rather than Bingley. According to Wilkinson, they were "sworn upon a book" and now "conferred together to make a lamina for invoking a spirit called Oberion" from a book provided by Wilkinson. This was to take place in a four-windowed room provided by Jameson. Sometime after the second Sunday in Lent, a witness named Henry Bank overheard them talking about their continuing efforts and reported hearing them say how Steward "was not so cunning as they were."

Progress was made more difficult because rumors had begun to spread about their activities. Wilkinson did not want to come to York, saying that their earlier meeting "had made a great rumor and slander in the country." On St. Mathias Day (February 22, 1510), Jameson rode to Bingley to tell Wilkinson that Richardson had made the lamina and everything was ready. Despite pressuring Wilkinson to complete the operations in York, Jameson said he could not be at the operations himself because of the rumors. Certainly, a number of other people in the vicinity of Bingley would have known something was up: the local farmer they paid to help find the cross, the people in Cockham where seven of them ended up, Greenwood's father and brother, and anyone else who had seen them. But perhaps more crucially, Wilkinson claimed that John Steward's involvement had made their activities particularly suspicious. This seems credible.

After this, Ottwell at Hagh claims to have ridden to the Bradford Fair (February 22–24, 1510) with Jameson but claims not to have talked about the matter. Whether more operations happened after that is unclear. The whole affair came to an inglorious end with a series of arrests and the seizure of the lamina and related books at York. Rumors of the treasure hunt, traveling "by public voice and fame," had evidently found their way to the authorities, who proceeded quickly to bring the culprits to justice.

THE ARCHBISHOP'S COURT

Although necromantic magic texts insist their power derives from the Christian status of the operator, his state of grace, and the power of God, the orthodox response was that what made the magic work (if it did at all) was an implicit or explicit pact made with the demons, sometimes involving some form of sacrifice or other religious homage. It was therefore a form of apostasy and certainly not orthodox Christian behavior. The notion of sacrifice, for example, lies behind the story that John Steward fed the "humble bees" (understood to be demons) with his own blood. Elsewhere, the Mixindale nine were accused of making sacrifices and prayers to demons. Archbishop Bainbridge's vicar general was especially troubled by rumors of clergy involved in conjuring demons, since clerical conduct was supposed to set an example for the laity. The records of the case do not include the positions, in which the commissary (canon lawyer) sets out the case against the accused. Nevertheless, the line of questioning in the examinations reveal that the major issue at stake was the participants' erroneous belief ("firm faith" as they call it) that magical powers could be used to control demons and, moreover, that the accused priests had spread these beliefs to others. These were heretical crimes.

Heresy was not merely a matter of believing the wrong thing. One also had to persist in those wrong beliefs in the face of correction by the church and to persist in publicly disseminating errors. People could only be turned over to the secular authorities for execution if they refused correction or if they had accepted correction and then returned publicly to their prior beliefs (thereby making themselves *relapsed* heretics). Because heresy threatened the salvation of the accused and others, it was a grave sin and the most serious accusation the church court could bring against an individual. Accepting correction meant your punishment would be public penance and possibly fines and imprisonment, depending on the gravity of the case. A second offense could mean the death sentence, which would be handed down in secular courts after the prisoner was turned over to them by church officials.[1]

Technically, the Mixindale fellowship could have been charged with practicing magic or with fraud, and while these would also have demanded penance, they did not carry with them the powerful requirement of never repeating the crime again without threat of being a relapsed heretic. In short, by excommunicating the Mixindale nine for heresy and subjecting them to protracted public penance, the archbishop's officials made it completely clear to everyone the gravity of the crime and that they would brook no repetition.

1. Caterina Bruschi and Peter Biller, *Texts and the Repression of Medieval Heresy*, York Studies in Medieval Theology (Woodbridge, UK: York Medieval Press; Rochester, NY: Boydell & Brewer, 2003); Malcolm Lambert, *Medieval Heresy: Popular Movements from the Gregorian Reform to the Reformation*, 3rd ed. (Oxford, UK: Blackwell, 2002).

REGISTER OF ARCHBISHOP BAINBRIDGE OF YORK[2]

3.1. Articles Presented Against Sir James Richardson, Priest

In the name of God, Amen. We, John Carver, doctor of laws, vicar general in spirtualities of the most reverend Father and Master in Christ, Lord Christopher, [who is] by the grace of God archbishop of York, primate of England and legate of the Apostolic See, being absent, propound and set out the subscripted articles and contents therein to you, Sir James Richardson who are a priest, publicly challenged concerning heresy or sorcery. You were taken under suspicion of heresy through the lay power, and handed over to us, for the genuine correction and health of your soul and the extirpation of this kind of crime and for no other purpose nor in any other way.

In the first place, we set out and propound to you that you are a priest, publicly and openly designated in the order of the priesthood.— He confesses the article.

Also, knowing that a certain John Steward of Knaresborough makes use of false and condemned conjurations, invocations, and sorceries, and that John Steward was publicly known and decried for such [practices], you consulted and have done business with the same John for recovering a stolen thing by means of his magic and condemned art, and for getting information about a certain Christopher Scaresborough lately the fugitive servant of Thomas Jameson.

Sir James, sworn and examined, responded and said that after the feast of the Epiphany just passed, while riding to Knaresborough with Thomas Jameson of York (which he did at Thomas's request), Thomas told him that he had heard that John Steward might lay bare information about his fugitive servant and about his stolen goods. Where, after Thomas told John the reason he had come, Thomas gave John 6 shillings and 8 pence and John promised that in the morning

2. York, Borthwick Institute for Archives, Abp. Reg. 26 Christopher Bainbridge (1509–1514), fols. 68r–72v; see also James Raine, "Proceedings Connected with a Remarkable Charge of Sorcery, Brought Against James Richardson and Others, in the Diocese of York, A.D. 1510," *Archaeological Journal* 16 (1859): 71–81.

he would show him where he might find his servant.—And among other things he confesses as articulated.

Also, that John Steward said and asserted to you that, because he had confessed last lent, he did not want to permit incantations or conjurations to be done in this case; and finally, he told you about a large hidden treasure in a certain place called Mixindale; he wished to make a plan, with your help and the help of others, unquestionably to recover it, because it would yield him more than a hundredfold profit.—He confesses to the article inasmuch as it is contained in the letter passed on to him by John, because, as he said, the effect of this article was contained in the letter sent to himself and to Thomas Jameson; but it did not designate in the letter the place where the treasure had been hidden.

Also, that you had faith in the words of John and steadfastly promised to be a part of his plan in that work, and you gave your advice for the purpose of obtaining the treasure, both through conjurations and invocations of daemons, and through other illicit and condemned divinations and sorcery.—He said that for the sake of greed he gave faith to the words of John, believing that the treasure would be discovered through art of this kind.

Also, that you made and caused to be made one instrument called "a lamina," fit for the work of conjuration, invocation, and sorcery, and other instruments necessary and best for the work, with the advice of others connected to you in this part.—He confessed that he had made a lamina that was made square from lead and it was sculpted with the image of a man, according to the information of Brother John Wilkinson, canon at Drax, who gave to him a book about the practice of this kind of art of conjuring. And he said that the lamina is an instrument for conjuration; and also he said that he handed over the book to the Mayor of the City of York with the aforementioned instrument.

Also, that you made or caused to be made one circle of virgin parchment, with characters and names and other superstitious signs; and that you preserved and kept the circle for the purpose of accomplishing work of this kind, just as you keep [it] in the present.—He confesses the article and says that John Steward gave virgin parchment of this type to him and that John got the virgin parchment from a certain Thomas Laton, dwelling in the bishopric of Durham, just as John has revealed in his article.

Also, he confesses that, in his following examination, he will be strongly suspected for invoking daemons.

Also, he says that he engraved the figure of Oberion the daemon in the lamina and 4 names, whereof Storax was one, and the other 3 after the book [68v].

Also, that in a certain place commonly called Mixindale Head below the parish of Halifax, on the 28th day of the month of January, in the year of the Lord 1509, with some other of your confederates, you *de facto* performed a work of this kind of conjuration, invocation, or sorcery; or at least it was not at your instigation that the work was conducted there, but you applied your diligence, as far as it was in you, for the purpose of accomplishing that work.—He says that he applied his diligence with Thomas Jameson of York, John Steward of Knaresborough, Sir John Wilkinson, Sir Richard Greenwood, Lawrence Knowles of Knaresborough, a certain Ottwell at Hagh from Bingley and his servant, and Thomas Wood of the same, that they should meet in the place called Mixindale for carrying out and employing the said work of conjuration; and nevertheless they were not able to gather at the same time, on account of the intervening night. And on the following day, Sir Richard led his father and brother with him unto Bingley, for the purpose of completing the work of this kind; and when Sir James Richardson and Thomas Jameson asserted that they did not want further with the work of this kind of conjuration, the father of Sir Richard desired Sir James to hand over the circle to him, which Sir James refused to hand over to him. And intemperately, Thomas Jameson sought the names of each one to be rendered in writing, and the father of the said Sir Richard, where he was [customarily] named Greenwood, made himself to be called Michelson.

Also, that then and there you invoked daemons, and you received their response for having the stolen item or hidden treasure.—He denies the article.

Also, that you made prayers and other sacrifices to daemons, or at least you were a part of the counsel of others doing this work and you were in their fellowship and company.—He denies the article.

Also, that you gave a firm faith to the work, prayers and sacrifices, characters, and others aforementioned; and indubitably you believed in them.—He denies the article.

Also, that you kept and wrote books of this kind of art and that you believed in them.—He denies the article.

Also, that you worked concerning the foregoing and it is public voice and fame, etc. [i.e., publicly gossiped about].—He agrees concerning the beliefs [of the public] and denies concerning the denials [i.e., continues to deny those items he denied above.]

Also, that you consulted John Steward about certain things removed by Edward Clifford long before Thomas Jameson made the request to you; and you rode with the said Thomas Jameson unto Knaresborough.—He confesses the article.

Also, that you received [and] preserved one book from Sir John Wilkinson, Canon of Drax, and another book of condemned readings from John Steward and you copied them.—He confesses the article that he possessed two books.

Also,[3] he, afterward examined, saith that he carried the singing breads to Bingley, and he and Jameson were agreed that two should be consecrated, one for himself, and another for Jameson, to be put upon them in time of conjuration to defend them from the spirit; and when they were at Bingley, Steward and Sir John showed that might not be,[4] for if[5] the sacrament were there, the spirit would not appear. And he saith that he never knew that the singing breads were at any time hallowed.

Also, he saith that he and Thomas Jameson made genuflections and said prayers at the making of the circle after[6] Steward's book; and also Steward gilded the scepter in Ottwell's chamber, and in likewise

3. Manuscript switches from Latin to Late Middle English here. It seems that the following two paragraphs were recorded after the initial examination at the presentation of the articles. Because this case is copied from earlier documents into the archbishop's register, we have no way of knowing if the scribe was copying directly or organizing material from separate sheets of parchment in the commissary's file.

4. I.e., that using the breads in this way wouldn't work.

5. for and

6. I.e., following the directions in Steward's book.

he and Jameson made kneeling and genuflections, and said prayers at the making of the lamina.

3.2. Articles Presented Against Thomas Jameson of York, Merchant

In the name of God, amen, just as above the articles have been written below, we set out [the case] against you Thomas Jameson, merchant of the City of York, etc., as above.[7]

In the first place, we propound and demonstrate to you that you, knowing that John Steward from Knaresborough used false and damnable conjurations, invocations of malign spirits, and sorcery, and that he had been named and defamed publicly for such things, you consulted and have done business with the same John for recovering a stolen thing by means of his magic and condemned art, and for having information about a certain Christopher Scarborough, lately your fugitive servant.— He says that because of the information of Sir James Richardson (who intimated to him that John Steward of Knaresborough was learned in such a way that he would get news of his fugitive servant for Thomas;) he rode with Sir James unto Knaresborough to John Steward [69r]. He said that he never heard before that John had made use of invocations of spirits, conjurations, or sorcery, nor about any infamy of this sort working additionally against him.

Also, that you gave and paid 6s 8d to John Steward, for information about your servant, and for incantations of demons, invocations, and other magic and condemned arts for the recuperation and restitution of other things furtively stolen by the same Christopher your servant and carried away with him.—He confesses that he gave one noble to John for gaining information about his servant, but he was entirely ignorant about what art, cunning, or method he used.

Also, that after receiving the money, John Steward asserted, "Let God, the devil, and me alone."—He confesses the article.

Also, that afterward John Steward informed you about a large hidden treasure in a certain place called Mixindale, concerning which,

---

7. Manuscript returns to Latin here.

with your help and [the help] of the two priests of Bingley, and of others in on his plan, he [i.e., John] wanted to work and to recover, undoubtedly, that [treasure].—He says that, at his first meeting, John Steward revealed [his plans] to Sir James Richardson, as was articulated. And that at his second meeting in Knaresborough in like manner he [i.e., John] reported to Thomas.

Also,[8] that you have put trust in the words and assertions of John, and you firmly promised to be of his counsel in that illicit work and you gave consent to the obtaining of the said treasure both through conjurations and invocations of demons and through other illicit and condemned divinations and sorceries.—He says that as soon as he heard that Sir John Wilkinson, canon regular, Sir Richard Greenwood, and John Steward were endeavoring to recover the treasure through the invocations of demons, conjurations, or other illicit means, he said that he did not want to meddle with them further in this cause, and, asking about the names of those who were present then, he sent them away and afterwards did not give faith to their words.

Also, that you, with others adhering to you in this part, offered consent to the fabrication of a certain instrument called a "lamina" apt for the work of conjuration of spirits, of invocation, and of sorcery, and the fabrication of other instruments necessary and best for the said work.—He said that he knew that Sir James Richardson had made a "lamina" with a circle through the instructions of one book given to him by Sir John[9] Wilkinson.

Also, that in a certain place commonly called Mixindale Head below the parish of Halifax on the 28th day of the month of January in the year 1509 with some other of your accomplices of this kind, *de facto* you have made a work of conjuration, invocation, or sorcery or at least it was not your fault that the said work was conducted there, but you employed your diligence to the extent that it was in you for the work.—He confesses that he took a trip to the said place for acquiring and recovering the treasure by good means with others walking with him, for the treasure; but nevertheless with the coming of night they

8. The next eight paragraphs were left out entirely from Canon Raine's transcription of Thomas Jameson's responses to the articles.

9. The scribe has written *Ricardus* in error.

did not reach the same place and that at no other time afterward did he employ any diligence in this cause.

Also, that you then and there invoked demons and you took their responses for having the stolen goods and the treasure.—He denies the article.

Also, that you made prayers and made other sacrifices to demons or at least from the counsel of others you worked these operations and you were a part of the counsel of others and of their number.—He denies the article.

Also, that you gave firm faith to the said work, prayers, and sacrifices, characters and other aforementioned things and that without a doubt you believed in them.—He denies the article.

Also, that you possessed, preserved, and wrote books of this kind of art and you believed in them.—Thomas Jameson denies this article, he says nevertheless that Sir James Richardson wrote one book conveyed to the same Sir James through the Canon [of Drax] and another book given to himself by John Steward.

Also, that every single aforementioned thing was known and manifest through the whole city and diocese of York and other places surrounding and these things were subject to public voice and fame that circulated and still circulates.—He believes about the believed things [i.e., agrees there were rumors] and denies about the denied things [i.e., denies all the things he has already denied].

Further, he says that Edmund Greenwood, alias Michael of Heptonstall, told him that a certain Lenthorp of Bradford, Watson de Wakefield, Halywell, a monk from Salley, saw beforehand the said treasure in the stated location.

3.3. Examination of William Wilson of Bingley[10]

William Wilson of Bingley, twenty-one years of age, sworn and examined, confesses and says that, Monday after Candlemas day, as he

10. Unless indicated otherwise, all the depositions are recorded in Late Middle English.

remembers, [there] met in the house of Ottwell at Hagh at Bingley nine persons, that is to say, Sir James Richardson, Sir John Wilkinson, Sir Richard Greenwood, Thomas Jameson, John Steward, Lawrence Knowles, Thomas Wood, the said Ottwell at Hagh, and this deponent [69v] William Wilson. There [they] concluded, by a whole consent, upon such information as they had afore of Sir Richard Greenwood and Sir John Wilkinson, that there was a chest of gold in Mixindale, and every noble as thick as five, and upon the same chest a sword of maintenance, and a book covered with black leather. There they were fully agreed to get the same, and Wilson said at that time to them all that he would consent thereto, so that it might be done with the laws of God.

Furthermore, at that meeting in the same house secretly, Sir John, Sir James, and Thomas Jameson went into a chamber and there opened two bags[11] upon a bed. Suddenly, the forsaid deponent came among them and saw a circle made of parchment, after his understanding. Also, they had a great mass book open afore them and wrote out what they would and he saith that the circle was twenty-one feet wide, as Sir James said. Also, he saw two stoles and a thing gilded of a foot long like a holy water strinkle, and frankincense, with diverse books of their craft.

Also, then and there the foresaid Sir John delivered unto this deponent twenty-eight singing loaves (and not hallowed as he said) and then this said deponent asked Sir John what he would do with them. He said that if[12] the spirit would not obey, that then he would consecrate them and hold them up before the spirit and it should appear to him like a child of two years old, and then he would obey.

Also, then they were agreed all to meet at a cross at Solen End at the sun setting on the Tuesday. In eschewing of suspicion, Sir Richard Greenwood and Wood feigned[13] to go together to Sir Richard's father's [home] to eat a hen and to meet them at the cross at that time. Sir James, Thomas Jameson, Steward, and Ottwell departed out of the said town at another end and Sir John at another end alone, and Knowles, and this said deponent at the end where[14] Sir John went after him.

---

11. *bogettes*
12. *and*
13. *feyned theyme*
14. *at*

Also, they all, except Sir Richard and Wood, met on a moor called Wilston Lee and suddenly [there] came upon them a great mist which caused them to go out of the way, and so [they] happened upon[15] a town called Cockham, a mile from the cross. There the forsaid Ottwell got fire and salt, and the said Ottwell had a torch end and another torch end was in the company, but he [i.e., Wilson] knew[16] not who had it.

Also, the said deponent saith that forsaid Sir James lost the holy water strinkle in the said moor.

Also, he saith that the said Sir James had a censer to cense with.

Also, he saith that after this they went to a cross on Micklemoss, a mile from the other Cross and there Sir John, Ottwell, and Knowles said that they would seek the other cross and so went from them and met with a man that dwelled within half a mile of it. They gave him two pence for his labor to bring them to it, and he and they sought it and could not find it. Then they returned again to the cross of Micklemoss,[17] and then the other four were departed to a town called Cockham, and there provided for their supper, and so were there all seven persons.

Also, then afterward departed to Bingley Sir John, Wilson, and Lawrence Knowles. On the way[18] they agreed that they should meet on the moor in Arden Wood.

Also, this Wilson and Knowles brought Jameson, Sir James, and Steward their horses at Cockham and showed them of that meeting and how Sir John said, by the way, that he would bring the gold to that wood by a spirit carrier.

Also, they all met there but Sir John and Wood. Then were they all angry [7or] with Sir John. The foresaid Sir Richard brought with him his father and his brother, and his father said to Jameson, "Sir, ye seem a gentleman, and I advise you, go not about this matter, but if ye have well learned men, for there have[19] been wise men and well learned afore times about it, and yet they could not get it." And he said

---

15. *to*
16. *wot*
17. Very likely this is present day Mixinden, but we have preserved the name used in the documents because

they refer to Mixindale Head as well as Mixindale.
18. *and in the waie going*
19. *has*

that he could show the names of the persons that had it of late years above the ground, and so on the morning Jameson wrote their names.

Also, the same morning, after great communication for division of the gold, Jameson said that every yeoman should have twenty pounds and he would have the remnant to York. The other party said, "Nay," for they would be all like in division. Then Jameson said, "Nay," and in anger said that he would show the King and his council of them and wrote their names in so much that Sir Richard's father changed his name and called [himself] Mitchell for fear, where his name was Greenwood.

3.4. Examination of Sir John Wilkinson, Canon of Drax

Sir John Wilkinson, canon of Drax, sworn and examined, confesseth and saith that he is a priest, and grievously defamed of heresy and conjurations, where through this ill weather comes.

Also, he saith that William Wilson was the first that showed him that there was a great good [i.e., treasure] in the country that might be got if there were any cunning men in the country.

Also, he saith he had communication with Steward of this matter before[20] he was acquainted with Jameson or Sir James.

Also, he saith that Steward sent to him a book of experience[21] and he sent him another by Lawrence. Then Steward sent that book to Jameson and Sir James to make a circle by. They made three, and this canon made one of them, all of thirty feet compass, and were agreed that eight should be within the circle and Steward without. The said canon was agreed to make the invocation and call up a spirit called Belphares.

Also, the said canon saith that when he was a child of twelve years of age he was at an invocation made at Wakefield by a scholar of Orleans for a pair of beads where he saw in a glass a woman that had the beads in her hand and a spirit crowned like a king in a chair of gold, and the clerk said that he was a spirit.

20. *afore or*

Also, he saith that he, Thomas Jameson, and Sir James, were sworn upon a book and conferred together to make a lamina for invocation of a spirit called Oberion for to have knowledge of Jameson's servant and his goods and to know whether there were any goods in Mixindale. Jameson was agreed to send a horse for him to Ottley, the Friday afore the first change of March, to come to York to him to make the lamina, which must be made betwixt the change of the moon and the prime that was Monday, Tuesday, and Wednesday and to make their invocation on Thursday after, at five of the clock in the morning at York in a chamber to be provided to the said Sir James, having four windows, that is to say, in every quarter one.

Item. He saith that he durst not come to York because of their meeting afore, which had made a great rumor and slander in the country, for so much as Steward was in their company. He sent to Thomas Jameson by one John Hardy a letter, desiring in the same to send a hour glass,[22] a dial with the needle[23] and a stone, which the said Jameson promised him afore.

Also, he said that Hardy met not with Thomas Jameson and so he had no dial nor glass.

Also, he saith that the afore written communication (of the making of the said lamina and other things to be done about the knowing both of the said servant [70v] and of the treasure) was at Bingley the same morning after the departing of the great company, upon displeasure and dissention they had amongst themselves there.

Also, the said Jameson came to Bingley upon Saint Mathias Day, fair time at Bradford, and showed him that Sir James had made all things ready and desired him [Wilkinson] to come to York and [that] Sir James and he [Wilkinson] should work the work, and he [Jameson] would be of consent but he would not be present, for there was a great rumor upon it as well at York as in the country.

Also, he confesseth that he had all his books at Drax Abbey.

Also, he confesseth that Sir James brought the 28 singing loaves from York, and this deponent delivered them to William Wilson. He saith they were never consecrated.

---

21. = experiments
22. *rynning glass*

23. *neld*, for use in a compass

Also, he denieth that ever he said that he would consecrate those singing loaves, nor that they should appear in the likeness of a child to the spirit. But he confesseth that all the whole company were agreed that the ground where the circle should be [be] hallowed, and also that Thomas Jameson or [someone] else did write out of the mass book a collect for the hallowing of the incense[24] and fire, and in their book of experiment was written the hallowing of the great holy water.

Also, he says that William Ottwell, alias Wilson, never said to him that he would not consent to the getting of the treasure except[25] if it might be done by the laws of God, nor [did he] put any exception; and he was the most laborious and solicitous[26] betwixt Steward and the said Sir John upon his own cost.

Also, he saith that he hath no more books than is delivered to my Lord Darcy.

Also, he showeth and confesseth that Sir Richard Greenwood brought his father to Bingley to show them to the ground where the treasure was.

Also, he saith that Sir Richard made [an] appointment with Lawrence and Wilson to meet at a wood called Arden, near unto Bingley. He confesseth that he said that their works might be done as well in one place as other for [he] could make the spirit Belphares carry it wherever he would.

Also, he saith that he said openly that the treasure[27] could not be had without loss of a Christian soul, and therefore he would not execute it.

Also, in all other things as in the meeting at Bingley, division on the moor, coming to Cockham, [for] fire [and] salt for making holy water, he agrees with Wilson.

3.5. Examination of Ottwell at Hagh

Ottwell at Hagh, of Bingley, 50 years of age, sworn and examined, saith that at the first knowledge that he had of the treasure in Mixindale was

---

24. *incensn*   26. *laboror and solicitor*
25. *but*   27. *goode*

by his servant William Wilson, and said that there was a clerk went walking about that believed[28] that he could provide them advantage[29] therein.

Also, he saith that when they went to the moor, he bore in his sleeve two torch ends, that his servant William bore censers in his sleeve, and Sir John a holy water strinkle. But he saith that he knew not for what cause these things were borne.

Also, he saith that Sir John showed unto him behind Richard Lange's garden[30] house, that this treasure might be had by the laws of God, and he said if[31] it so might be, he would be more glad to meddle therewith or else he would not meddle, and Sir John said, "It stands with the laws of God."

Also, he saith that at their departing on the Thursday in the morning Jameson would not suffer him to come into the chamber to see such stuff as he brought from York, he never saw none of their stuff, nor knew that there was any singing breads,[32] nor was of counsel of any conjuration for raising of spirits to be done. But he agreed to them at the first meeting to be one of them to go get this treasure.

Also, he saith he rode to Bradford fair with Thomas Jameson and neither that [71r] time nor afore he had communication with him of this matter but once, when Thomas Jameson desired him to come to York. But he knows[33] not wherefore nor he came not there.

3.6. Examination of Lawrence Knowles of Herrogate

Lawrence Knowles, de Herrogate, thirty-eight years of age, sworn and examined, saith that John Steward of Knaresborough was the first that showed him of the treasure in Mixindale and said that the two priests of Bingley showed him that it might be gotten with their three cunnings[34] by conjuration and invocation of spirits.

28. *trowed*
29. *vauntage*
30. *garth*
31. *and if*
32. *nor he never see noone of their stuff, nor he knewe not that there was any singing bredes*

33. *wottes*
34. I.e., the magical knowledge and abilities of Jameson, Greenwood, and Wilkinson.

Also, he confesseth that he brought letters from Steward to Sir James and bore a letter from Sir James to Steward and another letter from Steward to the two priests of Bingley, and there had communication with them of this treasure. They said it were a good deed to get that good with the power of God and he said that [if] it might be so with the laws of God and the laws of the crown, he would be content therewith and they said that it was not against the King because they would not break the ground.

Also, he confesseth that the priests showed them all that eight of them should be within the circle and one without. He saith that Ottwell knew that he prepared[35] salt for the making of holy water to defend them from spirits and Steward said that he would be without the circle, for he trusted so well in his cunning and was afraid of nothing.[36]

Also, he saith that Steward said to him that he delivered to Sir James virgin parchment to make the circle of.

Also, he saith that he, at Christmas last, brought to Sir James from Steward a shoulder of venison and a capon and at that time he had communication with Sir James and Jameson both of the treasure and of his good, and Jameson gave him twelve pence and made him of counsel.

Also, the priests, on Wednesday at evening, said that they would prepare[37] a little thing at Gillside, but Jameson would not consent thereto.

Also, at their departing upon the Thursday, Jameson was angry[38] with the priests and said that they mocked him, and there wrote a thing and said it were a good deed and it pleased the King to get cunning men from Orleans to get it.

3.7. Examination of Thomas Wood of Bingley

Thomas Wood of Bingley, thirty-five years of age,[39] confesseth and acknowledged himself to be defamed and slandered of heresy, and he

---

35. *sett*
36. *was no thing aferd*
37. *sett for*
38. *wrothe*
39. *annorum etatis*

saith that Sir Richard Greenwood was the first that he heard speak of the good in Mixindale.

Also, he saith that William Wilson showed him in like wise of that good and said that there were clerks that had books that could get it. He broke [it] to Sir Richard and showed him what Wilson had said, and he said that believed[40] that Sir John and he had books that would do good and they were occupied.

Also, he saith that was [a matter of] communication among them that the good must be gotten with the conjuration of spirits.

Also, he saith that when Steward and they of York came to Bingley, Sir Richard and Sir John sent for him to come to them, and so he did. They said to him that the men of York had come, and they would go about the getting of this good, and desired him to go with them, and so he granted. Then they said to him that he must come in the morning to the kirk and hear two masses and be shriven because the spirits should have no power of them. So, he came to the kirk and heard two masses, Sir James sang one and Sir Richard the other, and Sir Richard did shrive him going on the moor towards his father, that his father might bring them to the place. He meddled no more with them after this.

3.8. Examination of Sir Richard Greenwood, Chaplain

Sir Richard Greenwood, chaplain, examined by the Lord Vicar General Master Henry Machil, doctor of laws, lord official of the court of York, commissar general, and Master John Underwood, said[41] that the first knowledge of the matter that he is accused upon was by one William of Ottwell of Bingley, [who] told him, about Michaelmas last passed, that he pressed[42] Steward, clerk of Knaresborough, to come [71v] over to Bingley and for to bring his books with him if he trusted[43] to get knowledge through his books of any goods hidden in the ground. The said Steward came over to Bingley and brought with him Thomas Jameson of York and a priest of York, and one of Knaresborough, to

---

40. *trowed*
41. Paragraph in Latin to this point.

42. *made labor to*
43. *trowed*

Bingley and there lodged them at Ottwell's, master to the foresaid Ottwell [i.e., William Wilson] and he [i.e., Steward] sent for the said Sir Richard and Sir John and Thomas Wood and there he and they had communication where any good or treasure should be hidden in the earth. There they were agreed that there was a hoard in Mixindale, called Mixindale hoard and because he knew the way best thither he should bring them thither, and they were agreed that they should all meet at a cross at the west end of Sole Hill in Halifax parish, at the sun setting the same day, which is from the dale a mile. Thomas Wood and the said Sir Richard kept their appointment and all the others went out of their way and came not there by two miles, and so Steward, Ottwell, the priest of York, and Thomas Jameson were all night in Bradford Dale Head. Sir John, the canon, William Ottwell, and a little fellow from Knaresborough came to Bingley and the said Sir Richard and Wood came thither too and so the morrow next after they met all at Bingley and dined all together. When they had dined, they departed. He saith they all trusted to find the hoard, and he should have had part with them for bringing them to Mixindale, and the said Sir Richard saith that they intended to get that good with their books, but he was not of counsel with them of their books.

3.9. Examination of Sir Henry Bank, Chaplain of Addingham

Sir Henry Bank, chaplain of Addingham, a witness, introduced and sworn and diligently examined says that on a certain Sunday in Lent just past, the second Sunday as he believes, the same Henry was present in the house of Christopher Hardwick of Addingham, and then in that place Sir Henry heard brother John, the parish priest of Bingley, say publicly there[44] that there was as much good in a place beside Halifax as would ransom a king, and that one Leventhorp, now dead, had seen the foot of the chest and the devil sitting upon it, and that he put a sword to remove it and he nipped it asunder in the midst, as [if] it had been a rush. The said Sir John said it would never be got but with the loss of a Christian soul and Sir Richard Greenwood affirmed

---

44. Paragraph Latin to this point.

every word and the said Sir John and Sir Richard granted there that they and one Steward of Knaresborough had been at the ground and seen it and they said that Steward could do naught;[45] he was not so cunning as they were. Also, he saith that Sir William Hardwick, parish priest of Addingham, was there present and heard this and he saith also that one Sir Thomas Spurret of Pole, in the parish of Ottley, showed unto him that he saw Steward have three humble bees,[46] or like humble bees, and kept them under a stone in the earth, and he called them out by one and one and gave each one of them a drop of blood of his finger.

3.10. Examination of Sir Richard Greenwood

An examination of this kind was made on the 26th day of April 1510 AD, the parties then present being Sir Thomas Jemyson[47] and William Spenser chaplains and me John Deyce notary public.[48]

Sir Richard Greenwood examined again saith and confesseth the saying of Thomas Wood in part of his last deposition and that Steward said that all should be in the circle, but he and he would be sometimes within and sometimes without. He feared no thing.

Also, he saith that his father advised them not to meddle with this matter for they could never bring it about, but in every way[49] the world would wonder upon them. He confesses that he and his company [have] been slandered through all the country of heresy, and that their doing is the cause of all this ill weather.

Also, he confesses that he made the appointment of meeting in Arden Wood, and should have given Sir John warning in the morning and did not [72r].

Also, they all say that Steward was [of] counsel with them of fetching of fire and salt, and Sir James says that Steward gilded the scepter.

---

45. *noght do*
46. I.e., bumble bees.
47. Not Thomas Jameson mayor, but a different man.

48. This paragraph was recorded in Latin, the remainder in ME.
49. at all

3.11. Examination of John Steward of Knaresborough

John Steward of Knaresborough, forty-eight years of age, sworn and examined, saith that he has dwelled in Knaresborough by the space of sixteen years and some time taught grammar there. He saith that about this time twelve months ago[50] the two priests of Bingley, Sir John, the canon, and Sir Richard Greenwood, did send letters to him, showing him that there was good hidden in Mixindale, and if he would do as they would do, he should be partner with them and such other as they had of counsel to get it (which letters he delivered to my Lord Darcy's servants) and so, sore and many times labored by them, [he] granted to Ottwell's servant to come to them to Bingly and do as they did in the law of God, to live and die for it. They said that Robert Leventhorp had been in hand with it afore time.

Also, he saith that the priests would have had a portable altar[51] and said the mass in the house where they were lodged.

Also, he saith that Sir James came to him to have knowledge of certain goods stolen, and he showed him how the priests of Bingley labored him to be one of them for getting of the good in Mixindale, and Sir James said he would be glad to get it and promised to be one of them.

Also, he saith that Thomas Laton came once to him to Knaresborough to seek a remedy for a vexation that he had in his mind by night and by day. His kinsman Paule showed him that the said Laton had used invocations afore and brought him a book of Laton's that he calls a "speculatif" but he delivered it [to] him again incontinently. He saith that the book was of astronomy.[52] He saith that Laton was well eased by such things as he gave him in medicines of spices and herbs and words of God together, which was the gospel on the Ascension Day. He says that he believes steadfastly that these things, with other prayers and good deeds that he bid him do, did ease him. Also, he saith that when persons and people came to him to have knowledge of things lost and stolen, he would show them a book of astronomy and make them believe that he was cunning. He could do no thing,[53] but

---

50. *twelmonethe*
51. *superaltare*

52. See chapter 4.
53. *no thing do*

sometimes it happened, as he said, and that was as the blind man cast his staff,[54] and some would give him money, and some wax, wherewith he kept certain lights in the church.[55]

Also, he saith that he was at Bingley with his company as [it] was going to the place as they were, and he heard them speak that they had a holy water strinkle which was lost, and a censer, and frankincense, and other stuff ready. He saw them have a scepter, but he saw not the crown, but he saw two bags[56] that the stuff was in.

Also, he saith that he, Jameson, Sir James, Ottwell, and his servant came to the wood on the moor, where Sir John had promised to bring the good to by a spirit carrier. Sir Richard and his father and his brother came thither, and Sir John did not. Thence afterwards at Bingley, Jameson and Ottwell's servant fell out for the sword of maintenance and the good as the said servant showed him, and after that he was never of counsel with them.

3.12. Questions and Interrogation Put to the Same John Steward of Knaresborough[57]

In the first place, he was asked how long he had been involved with the invocation of spirits.—John Steward says that he had not been involved with the invocation of demons or spirits at any time, but said that he had once used the art of knowing stolen and lost goods by the turning of the key in the book while saying the psalm "*Deus Deorum* [72v], *Dominus locutus est*" with the versicle "*Si videris furem,*" etc.[58]

He was asked whether he believed according to the determination of the holy mother church.—He says that he believes.

---

54. I.e., like the blind man who hit his target by accident.

55. It is not unreasonable to assume that he had difficulty making ends meet and tried to supplement his income (and even funds for the care of the church) in this way.

56. *bogettes*

57. The interrogation articles are in Latin.

58. Ps 49:18 (Vulg.)

He was asked from whom he had his books of damned reading.—He says that he had one booklet from a canon and more he did not have.

He was asked whether he gave one book to Sir James Richardson and another book to a canon.—He says that he gave the said booklet to Sir James and that he did not give the canon any book.

Also, he was asked whether he said or heard another person saying that this chest could not be possessed without the perdition of one soul.—He says that he never heard anyone say [anything] as articulated.

He was asked whether he has three bumblebees and that they come at his call and he gives blood to them and afterwards they leave.—He denies the article.

Also, he confesses that he had received one noble from Thomas Jameson according to what was deposed above.

He was asked whether he made an instrument called a "lamina."—He denies this, and, concerning the three circles of parchment that had been made, he said that he did not make the circle, but gave the virgin parchment to Sir James Richardson. He says that the parchment is called virgin parchment because it is of the first calf that a cow has and he says that he had that parchment from a certain Thomas Paul, a cousin dwelling in Cleveland—but he says he cannot tell where—about 3 years ago.

Also, [asked whether] he baptized a cock, cat, or other animal.—He says not and he says that he did not make a sacrifice.

Also, asked whether anyone was able to invoke demons and whether he had ever invoked any demon.—He says that he never invoked a demon, and nor did he hope to be able to invoke [one].

He was asked why he had not heard mass at Bingley, as others had heard.—He says that he had been vexed with gout and therefore on account of the pain could not go to church at that same place.

Also, asked whether he had made confession and to whom.—He says that he had not made confession.

He was asked whether Sir James Richardson or another presbyter had consecrated some hosts and for what reason.—He says that he did not know about consecration nor did he see loaves nor know about them.

He was asked why he himself was outside the circle rather than the others.—He says that he cared not whether he were without the circle or within. And he was asked why he rather than the others. He says that he thinks himself so steadfast in the faith of the church that he feared nothing.

He was asked whether all these nine persons had consented to bringing about the nefarious act.—He says, "Yes."

Also, [asked whether], according to the design of his books, he said or wrote that holy confession in the time of Lent would not permit conjurations or invocations of demons to be made.—John Steward says that he sent word by Lawrence Knowles to Sir James Richardson that confession in Lent would not suffer invocation to be made but he remembers not that he wrote it.

[Also asked] whether there were any others of counsel than the nine persons named above.—He says, "No."

Also, [asked] whether Thomas Laton was of his counsel.—He says, "No."

Also, he confesses to have cultivated rumors concerning the above against that one and his allies named previously.

3.13. The Vicar General of York Commissions the Examination of John Steward, 12 May 1510

John Carver, doctor of laws, archdeacon at York in the metropolitan church at York, vicar general in spiritualities of the most reverend Father and Lord in Christ, Lord Christopher, by the grace of God, archbishop at York, primate of England, and legate of the Apostolic See, sends greeting in the Lord to the venerable Father in Christ, John, by the grace of God, bishop of Nigropont, suffragan of the said most reverend Father, and to Master Richard Newith, bachelor of laws.[59] Because, as we have heard, John Steward de Knaresborough of the dioceses of York (who is gravely defamed over sortilege and other illicit, erroneous articles damned through the determination of

---

59. Bachelor in Canon Law; also called Bachelor of Decrees.

Holy Mother church, and who is suspected over heretical distortion) has been transferred to prison custody at Pontefract through the lay power; therefore, for hearing and examining the cause or the affair of the heretical distortion, and for knowing, and proceeding, pronouncing and discerning upon the same, with all and single incurring, depending, coming forth and whatever matters are connected; and for doing, exercising, and settling all and singular other matters which will have been necessary or in any way appropriate in the foregoing and thereabouts [73r], we commit to you, through the present letter, jointly and severally, our standing with power of canonical reprimand of whatever kind; and duly you will inform us concerning all that which you have done and have found, before the last day of the month of May now instant, or thus let another associate of yours inform us, who in person shall have carried out our mandate. Given at York under the seal of our office aforesaid on the 12th day of the month of May in the year of our Lord 1510.

3.14. The Vicar General of York Requisitions the Mayor of York to Deliver James Richardson from the Civic Jail to the Prison of the Archbishop, 5 May 1510

[73r] John Carver, doctor of laws, etc., sends greetings to the notable and distinguished John Shaw, mayor of the city of York, beloved to us in Christ and showing due and readymade obedience to the business of the Catholic faith. Because, by faith worthy report and public fame circulating, it has rather frequently reached our hearing that Sir James Richardson, a priest, of the city of York, and Thomas Jameson, merchant, of the same city, and other diverse persons in the jurisdiction of the most reverend Father who are known, lying under, and suspected with a view to heretical depravity and other illicit condemned, erroneous doctrines, and who are gravely defamed, and arrested upon the same infamy, were taken and remanded into prison by your authority.

Truly, according to the duty of our office, to the glory of God and the augmentation of faith, we are bound, as much as is in us, to reform and stamp out the erroneous opinions and damnable and heretical doctrines of the said persons; and desiring to trust to the salvation of their souls, we require and urge in the Lord that, just as you desire to be reckoned and be known a faithful orthodox person, for the defense of the faith, you should turn your attention upon the diligent investigation, apprehension, and guard of the said persons (having been defamed for heretical depravity as was stated above) and of their promoters, shelterers, and defenders; and that you make to be led and to be freed the aforesaid pestiferous persons into the power and prison of the said most reverend Father at York (with the books and writings of condemned teaching and doctrine and other illicit tokens, if any have been found with the same persons) where they will be held in custody, skillfully and diligently, through us, vicar general in spiritualities of the same most reverend Father and other orthodox men, until their case will be determined through the judgment of the Church according to canonical sanctions and the statutes and provisions of this illustrious kingdom of England set forth in this case; and prohibiting you, especially, and other lords temporal and their officials and ministers in kind, lest you yourselves inquire or judge or they inquire or judge in whatever way concerning this crime, since it is purely ecclesiastical, or if you should free or they should free the captives for the same crime without the license of the said reverend Father or ours; nor, under pain of law, should you impede or they impede, directly or indirectly, the process against the aforesaid defamed persons through making an ordinary judgment or sentence. Also, we make it known to you that we wish to enjoin full faith to be given by you to John Chapman, notary public, bearer of these letters, our messenger sworn in this matter, concerning the delivery of these same letters. Given at York under the seal of our office aforesaid on the 5th day of the month of May in the year of the Lord 1510.

3.15. Record of a Letter to Lord Darcy, 7 May 1510

Also, on the seventh day of the month of May in the year of the Lord stated above, a copied letter was made and was directed to the nobleman Lord Thomas Darcy for the delivery of John Steward of

Knaresborough and of other persons defamed for heretical distortion, captured by the same Sir Thomas Lord Darcy and remanded to prison at the castle of Pontefract, etc.

3.16. Confessions and Assignment of Penance to All Except John Steward, 31 May 1510

And after the examinations of the said persons and the confessions of the same written above before the venerable man Master John Carver, doctor of laws, archdeacon at York, and vicar general in spiritualities of the most reverend Father and Master in Christ, Lord Christopher, by the grace of God, archbishop of York, primate of England, and legate of the Apostolic See being absent, and made in the presences of the venerable Masters James Harington, deacon of the metropolitan Church of York, William Melton, professor of sacred theology, Chancellor Robert Langton, doctor of both laws, the sacrists of the said church, Henry Machel, doctor of law, lord official of the court of York, the commissar general, and John Withers, master of art, canon in the churches of the cathedrals [73v] of St. Paul London and Salisbury, and the secretary of the said most reverend Father, the commissar and receiver general in the consistory of the same most reverend Father in the Cathedral church at York, sitting in public; the aforesaid Thomas Jameson, Sir James Richardson, Sir John Wilkynson, Sir Richard Greenwood, Ottwell at Hagh, William Wilson, Thomas Wood, Laurence Knolles on the Friday morrow after the feast of Corpus Christi, namely the last day of the month of May in the year of the lord Lord 1510, appearing personally confessed that they and each one of them were publicly defamed and suspected of the invocation of demons and of other articles confessed by them and each one of them, as stated, and they humbly surrendered themselves to the correction and command of the Church for their undertakings of this kind; and they sought the benefit of absolution from the sentence of major excommunication, which they incurred on the occasion of the aforementioned, and with a corporal oath preformed by each and every one of them, and with sufficient warranty having been furnished to obey the law and to fulfill the penance that would be enjoined to them all for the aforesaid manner of their sins, the venerable Master John Carver, vicar general in spiritualities, archdeacon, absolved all of them from a sentence of major excommunication, which on the occasion of the aforementioned indictment they all incurred lawfully. And in the part of their penance he caused and mandated all of them to be delivered from the prisons of the said most reverend Father at York and also he assigned to them the first Tuesday following immediately after the feast of St. William for receiving penance in return for their sins of this sort.

3.17. Public Penance of All Except John Steward, 11 June 1510

And indeed on that first Tuesday after the feast of St. William (namely on the eleventh day of the month of June in the year of the Lord aforementioned) having arrived, the venerable Master John Carver, vicar general in spiritualities, sitting publicly for trial in the consistory, imposed upon Sir James Richardson of York, Sir Richard Greenwood and Sir John Wilkinson of Bingley priests, Thomas Jameson of York Merchant, Ottwell at Hagh, William Wilson, Thomas Wood of Bingley and Laurence Knowles of Harrogate for their crimes and offenses concerning the invocation of demons and sortilege perpetrated by them, as previously stated, the penance written below as part of their penance; namely that Sir James, Sir Richard, and Sir John Wilkinson on the next following Sunday between the 10th and 11th hours a.m. of the same day, with bare feet, uncovered heads, by proceeding from the metropolitan church of York through the neighborhood called Petergate to the door of the house of the Carmelite brothers of the city of York, by carrying three banners to this door with certain characters and images depicted, they should proceed around the market above the Pavement of the aforenamed city and through the streets of Eastgate, Conyngstrete, and Stangate, humbly to receive the disciplines from the hands of the deacon of the Christianity of the city of York, at the doors of the metropolitan church of York, and of the house of the Carmelite brothers, and of the church of the parish of All Saints above the Pavement, and of the house of the Augustinian brothers of the same city, in the manor of penitents through everything.

And that Thomas Jameson by carrying a scepter, Ottwell at Hagh a lighted torch, William Wilson, a holy water strinkle, Thomas Wood, a thurible with incense, and Laurence a cerge with salt over top, upon staffs and by proceeding and going also through the abovenamed neighborhoods on the said Sunday and between the aforesaid hours let them proceed around the market in the way and form and places aforementioned, humbly to receive disciplines from the hands of the deacon of the Christianity of the city of York, in the manner of penitents through all. And that in similar mode and form the persons named above, let them go before the procession around the metropolitan church at York on the next Sunday following, and the remainder of their penance the aforesaid vicar general in spiritualities has reserved for himself, until the Friday next before the feast of the nativity of St. John the Baptist. Indeed, on which Friday having arrived, with the penance having been completed humbly and devoutly, the aforesaid vicar general in spiritualities enjoined to the abovenamed persons that a similar penance be humbly carried out and duly fulfilled in the aforementioned method and form around the aforesaid church of Bingley on Sunday next after the feast of the Apostles Peter and Paul [74r].

3.18. Public Penance of John Steward, August 1510

And on Thursday nearest before the feast of St. Laurence[60] in the year of the Lord 1510, the aforesaid Master John Carver vicar general in spritualities aforesaid, absolved John Steward of Knaresborough from a sentence of major excommunication, which he incurred on the occasion of the previous indictment, and having guaranteed, with a corporal oath having been offered first by him to obey the law and commandments of the Church and to perform the penance to be enjoined upon him for his offenses, and he [i.e., Carver] enjoined a penance to him, namely that he would carry one of the aforementioned banners in the method and form detailed above for three days on market days on Saturday around the market center of

60. August 10th.

York and the market center of Knaresborough and on the two Sundays following thereafter around the parish churches of the villages of Knaresborough, Ripon, and Doncaster, by walking before the processions in the method and form described above, in the way of penitence through all, etc.

CHAPTER 4

Treasure Hunting

The Magic Texts

The Mixindale treasure hunters employed a number of magic books and had even more at their disposal. Steward had access to books owned by Laton, including an astronomical work called a "speculatif." This seems likely to have been the *Speculum astronomiae*, which includes a discussion of magic texts in chapter 11.[1] Wilkinson said he would conjure the demon Belphares to bear treasure to Arden Wood. He almost certainly had the same text as is found in Scot's *Discoverie of Witchcraft*.[2] Richardson, Jameson, and Wilkinson were also "sworn upon a book," which was undoubtedly the *Sworn Book of Honorius* (*Liber iuratus Honorii*), a book held in the library of York Austin Friars to which Wilkinson would have had access.[3] The most significant to their operations appears to have been the *Treasury of Spirits* (*Thesaurus spirituum*). The operations undertaken in York by Wilkinson, Jameson, and Richardson after the dissolution of the fellowship included the construction of a four-windowed room, which is distinctive to that work:

1. Paola Zambelli, *The Speculum Astronomiae and Its Enigma: Astrology, Theology, and Science in Albertus Magnus and His Contemporaries*, Boston Studies in the Philosophy of Science 135 (Dordrecht; Boston: Kluwer Academic, 1992). See also Klaassen, *Transformations of Magic*, 33–56; Nicolas Weill-Parot, *Les "images astrologiques" au Moyen Âge et à la Renaissance* (Paris: Honoré Champion, 2002), 59–62.

2. Scot, *Discoverie of Witchcraft*, 415–20 (book 15, chap. 13). Since this text is widely available, we have not reproduced it here.

3. This text is widely available in both English and Latin and so we have not reproduced it here. Gösta Hedegård, ed., *Liber iuratus Honorii—A Critical Edition of the Latin Version of the Sworn Book of Honorius* (Stockholm: Almovist & Wiksell International, 2002). For the magic books at York Austin Friars, see Klaassen, *Transformations of Magic*, 65–77.

> Therefore, you should have a room, secret, bright, and square, in all four sides of which shall be a window one cubit in width or a little more. Let the room be situated thus: that one window be towards the east, one towards the west, one towards the south, one towards the north. And let the room be at least 20 feet wide or at most 30 feet wide.[4]

The subsequent operations in the *Thesaurus spirituum* include treasure hunting, so the book certainly would have attracted their interest. Other elements in their operations also confirm that they were probably using this text or material redacted from it.

Immediately prior to the ill-fated expedition to the moor, they prepared a scepter, and the cunning man John Steward said of this occasion that "he saw not the crown, but he saw two bags the stuff was in," implying that a crown was also part of the equipment in the bags. The *Thesaurus spirituum* requires the preparation of a scepter, crown, sword, and ring. Although the examinations do not record the last two items, these could certainly have been in the bags as well. The short passage for the preparation of a scepter (Text 4.1) is drawn from an English redaction of *Thesaurus spirituum* but lacks the "gilding" the treasure hunters evidently felt was required for this item.[5] While the *Thesaurus spirituum* contains a variety of treasure-hunting operations, these do not include one for getting demons to bring the treasure to the magician. It also does not include parchment circles or a lamina for invoking Oberion. These operations would have come from yet other sources. Richardson's idea of using consecrated hosts for protection does not appear anywhere in necromantic texts.

The treasure hunters' particular approach to magic circles is unusual for a number of reasons. First, most necromantic manuals instruct the magician to draw circles on the ground with a sword or

---

4. London, Wellcome Library, Wellcome 110, fol. 62v. Translated from Latin. For this passage in other versions of the *Thesaurus spirituum*, see London, British Library, Sloane 3853, fol. 12, and Oxford, Bodleian Library, e Mus 238, fol. 7v. A four-windowed room also appears in other conjuring manuals, such as Oxford, Bodleian Library, Rawlinson D. 252, fol. 107v and e Mus 173, fol. 41v.

5. For another operation from the *Thesaurus spirituum* with a scepter, see Klaassen and Bens, "Achieving Invisibility," 1–14.

with chalk and a piece of string, or to make it from ashes, stones, or sand.[6] Operations with parchment circles are relatively rare and appear to be a practical innovation, particularly useful for treasure hunting during which one would probably not have the time or opportunity to find clear or level ground and create a circle in other ways. Only two surviving early modern British manuscripts include instructions for magic circles made with parchment (Texts 4.4 and 4.5). An illustration in an early modern German manuscript makes clear that this technology was more widespread.[7] Second, necromantic texts uniformly insist that the conjurer and all his companions must be separated from demons by the circle. Most frequently, they stand inside the circle for protection from demons, and this is the case in Texts 2.3, 4.3, and 4.5. In some cases, this arrangement is reversed, with the demon inside the circle and the operator(s) outside, and in others spirits are given their own circle to appear in within a larger circle.[8] In any case, circles served to isolate the spirits and protect the magician. It is therefore curious that the Mixindale Fellowship assumed, at least in their initial operations, that Steward had to stand outside the circle, a matter to which we will return.

The Mixindale Fellowship's books also evidently included at least two forms of demon conjuration directly applicable to treasure hunting: one for casting out demons and the other for getting a demon to bring the treasure to the operator. Henry Bank's deposition (Text 3.9) relates a story that a certain Leventhorp once had seen the treasure but that the demon protecting it bit off the end of his sword and drew the treasure further underground. This kind of story was not uncommon. Local legends and literature regularly describe how mythical beasts or spirits guarded treasures, and the conjuring literature, which assumed these guards to be demons, commonly provided operations to deal

6. Kieckhefer, *Forbidden Rites*, 170–85. For chalk circles in the *Thesaurus spirituum*, see Wellcome 110, fol. 34v. For other examples, see Cambridge, University Library, Additional 3544, p. 23, and London, British Library, Harley 2267, fol. 32v. The *Liber iuratus Honorii* marks circles in sand and stones (Hedegård, *Liber iuratus*

Honorii, 119 [12: 1–5]) and with ashes (111 [101: 1]).

7. London, Wellcome Library, Wellcome 1466, fol. 14r.

8. London, Wellcome Library, Wellcome 110, fol. 12r, illustrates a circle in which the spirits are supposed to appear.

with them.[9] Precisely what the treasure hunters planned to do on the moor is not made clear in their examinations, but they seem to have believed that the treasure was located under a cross and guarded by a demon. This being the case, they would have needed an operation that would get the potentially harmful demon out of the way. Text 4.2 is an example of this common sort of operation. After the failure of this first effort, they decided to meet in Arden Wood where John Wilkinson would conjure a demon to bring them the treasure. Text 4.3 is one example of this common type of operation.[10]

After the dissolution of the Mixindale Fellowship, Wilkinson, Jameson, and Richardson began a new round of operations, which included the use of the four-windowed room from the *Thesaurus spirituum* and the oath from the *Sworn Book of Honorius*. Their principal goal was to get more information about the treasure, and for this they employed a lamina to invoke Oberion. James Richardson confessed that he had made this square item "sculpted with the image of a man, according to the information of Brother John Wilkinson." He engraved "the figure of Oberion, the daemon, in the lamina and 4 names, whereof Storax was one, and the other 3 [names] after the book." This was drawn from a common operation to acquire knowledge from Oberion (Text 4.6).[11] Conjuring texts assume that demons are organized in hierarchies, and this text seeks to control Oberion directly and also through his counselors, one of which was Storax. Although the name is suggestive of Oberon, the mythical king of the fairies who appears

---

9. Johannes Dillinger, *Magical Treasure Hunting in Europe and North America: A History* (New York: Palgrave Macmillan, 2012), 53–84.

10. See, for example, Oxford, Bodleian Library, Rawlinson D. 252, fols. 157v–159r. Also, Additional 36674 passage. The technique is mentioned in the *Thesaurus spirituum*. See London, British Library, Sloane 3853, fol. 28v.

11. The text below is drawn from Sloane 3318, fols. 18v–21r. Oxford, Bodleian Library, e Mus 173, fol. 72, contains a similar operation. The association of Oberion with treasure hunting is made in Washington, Folger Shakespeare Library, Vb 28, where he is said to be able to bear treasure out of the sea (p. 80) and to be one of Oberion's counselors (p. 195). Numerous other texts include conjurations for Oberion for various purposes, including Cambridge, University Library, Additional 3544, pp. 154–63; London, British Library, Sloane 3826, fols. 98r–99r; Sloane 3846, fols. 102v–106r; Wellcome 110, fol. 97r; and Rawlinson D. 252, fols. 139r–142v and 143v–156v.

in Shakespeare's Midsummer Night's Dream, here and elsewhere in the literature he is presented as a demon.[12]

Treasure hunting is perhaps the most common form of magic recorded in scores of late fifteenth- and sixteenth-century English magic manuscripts. So it is striking when a consistent combination of otherwise unrelated texts appears on multiple occasions.[13] The early seventeenth-century manuscript from which Texts 4.2 to 4.4 are drawn contains versions of virtually all the operations undertaken by the Mixindale treasure hunters: extracts from the *Thesaurus spirituum*, the lamina for invoking Oberion, operations to clear the ground of demons, operations to have demons extract and transport treasure, and instructions for a parchment circle.[14] The account of William Stapleton summarized in the general introduction similarly includes *exactly* the same constellation of sources and equipment. All of this suggests that there may have been a certain consistency of opinion among the community of practicing magicians about what the best equipment and operations for treasure hunting were.

The magic practices of the Mixindale Fellowship were also drawn from other sources. Most conjuring manuals are not made up of a single work but rather are compilations of different sorts of operations that could be combined for ad hoc uses.[15] These included not only

12. On Oberon the fairy and Shakespeare, see Barbara A. Mowat, "Prospero's Book," *Shakespeare Quarterly* 52, no. 1 (2001).

13. Examples of necromantic treasure hunting are found throughout this introduction. Other techniques include the use of a "magneticall rodd," or hazel wand. See, for example: Sloane 3846, fol. 25v; Sloane 3318, 34v; or Sloane 3822, fol. 84r–84v. For a very general survey of this literature, see Dillinger, *Magical Treasure Hunting*.

14. The Mixindale treasure hunters certainly did not use Oxford, Bodleian Library, e Mus 173, since it was copied in the latter part of the sixteenth century at the earliest. But it seems they may well have had an earlier copy

of a similar or related collection since it contains operations and instructions that bear striking resemblance to what we see in this case. In addition to the passages below, the volume has numerous operations for treasure (e.g., fols. 48r–49r and 64), two specifically for treasure in the sea (fols. 22r–23r and 29r–30r), one for removing demons that protect a treasure (fols. 39v–40r), and one for preventing anyone else from getting the treasure you are after (fols. 40v–41r). Remarkably, this volume also includes a section originating in the *Thesaurus spirituum* that demands the operator employ a four-windowed room, fol. 41v.

15. Klaassen, *Transformations of Magic*, 115–55.

conjurations of various kinds, but also prayers, liturgical elements, or biblical passages for use in the rituals. William Wilson (Text 3.3) reported that the priests copied a consecration out of a mass book in advance of their operations on the moor. They appear to have used the mass book to create an operation that their book required but for which it did not provide a script, something that is reflected in other necromantic manuals.[16]

Even popular or literary constructions of the necromancer seem to have informed their operations. The peculiar notion, recorded in Stewart's examination, that the magician should stand outside the circle while his compatriots were protected inside of it highlights yet another source for their magic. As we have seen above, the manuscripts of magic never suggest this arrangement. They may use the circle as protection for the magician and his compatriots or they may use it as a focus of power or even a location in which spirits might appear. By contrast, the pattern of the magician protecting his compatriots while standing outside is relatively common in literary and artistic representations of conjuring magic. For example, in his stories of necromancers, Caesarius of Heisterbach commonly has an unprotected magician place those watching his conjuration inside a protective circle.[17]

The influence of literary representations of magicians on the Mixindale Fellowship is also reflected in the figure of the clerk of Orleans. Wilkinson describes him as a real magician who had employed him as a child scryer. However, there is no historical reason to associate Orleans with conjuring. On the contrary, the idea seems to derive from the works of Chaucer, where the Clerk of Orleans appears in "The Franklin's Tale." Similarly, stories of boy scryers employed by magicians also appear in literary sources.[18] Thus it may be that the

---

16. The author of the Boxgrove Manual had to do just this when his main source text did not provide a consecration for a sword. Ibid., 102.

17. Caesarius of Heisterbach, "Dialogus miraculorum," in *The Dialogue on Miracles*, ed. Henry von Essen Scott and C. C. Swinton Bland (London: Routledge, 1929), 318–19.

18. Kieckhefer, *Forbidden Rites*, 170–76; John of Salisbury, "Policraticus," in *Frivolities of Courtiers and Footprints of Philosophers: Being a Translation of the First, Second, and Third Books and Selections from the Seventh and Eighth Books of the Policraticus of John of Salisbury*, trans. Joseph B. Pike (Minneapolis: University of Minnesota Press, 1938), 146–47.

story was entirely or partly concocted, or that Wilkinson used these known stories to weave what he thought would be a credible story. He clearly had a long interest in magic, and perhaps the suggestion that he had been drawn into it as a boy (although certainly credible) was a way of making it seem somewhat less sinister. Wilkinson might also have been protecting other magicians who were friends. Where the truth lies remains unclear, but the lines between his story and these literary constructions seem very hazy.

Magic manuscripts also informed or confirmed the way magicians acted and thought about themselves. Necromantic manuals were written by and for men and, as we have said above, tend to reflect masculine fantasies, goals, and anxieties. They also paint a flattering masculine picture of the magician and his compatriots as resolved, brave, loyal, and stout hearted. In fact, contact with women actually threatened the cultivation of magical power and one's ability to control demons. Excluding women and avoiding their company was undoubtedly a by-product of the clerical origins of necromancy, but it also played to the construction of necromancy in the secular realm.

The members of the Mixindale Fellowship certainly recognized and identified with the mythic construction of the male magician in magic books. In his examination, John Wilkinson, priest and canon from the Austin priory at Drax, claimed that he along with Thomas Jameson and James Richardson "were sworn upon a book." This book must have been *Sworn Book of Honorius*, which describes an ideal community of magicians and gives the rules to which they must all swear in order to be members.[19] The versions of this book preserved in England include a variety of complicated spirit-summoning operations, treasure hunting among them. However, the book requires a demanding seventy-two-day initiatory ritual. Had members of the Mixindale fellowship performed this, it seems probable it would have been mentioned. Nonetheless, the *Sworn Book* influenced them in a different way. It describes a close-knit group of men sharing in the holy wisdom of magic, united by deep friendship, and loyal to each other unto death. The oath they swore upon the book was thus far more than

19. Hedegård, *Liber iuratus Honorii*, 16 (1: 20–29).

an oath of secrecy. It was a declaration that they believed themselves to be part of an elite brotherhood of solemn, loyal, dedicated, wise, and learned magicians.

Treasure hunting was also clearly a masculine affair, at least in those cases that involved genuine efforts at conjuring demons and expeditions into fields and forests to dig.[20] This is in full evidence in the case of the Mixindale Fellowship, which was an exclusively male group. The mythology of treasure hunting that preceded them and their own reported exploits were replete with masculine signifiers: the story of Leventhorp and his associates seeing the chest and having his sword broken off by a demon, the resolute group of conspirators dedicated to dark purposes, the courageous expedition onto the desolate moor at night, the domination of demons, the bravery and bravado involved, and the "bragging rights" they would have had if they had succeeded. Their undertaking has all the trappings of the masculine game of poaching, which was also a largely male affair. Like treasure hunting, the payoff from poaching was also potentially high, as venison was a high-status meat. The piece of venison John Steward gave to James Richardson to encourage him to get involved in their scheme suggests Steward was also involved in the risky masculine economy of poaching.[21] So taken as a whole, the manuscripts and court records paint a coherent picture of necromancy, especially necromantic treasure hunting, as a peculiarly male form of folly.

20. The possibly fictional account of Judith Philips is a rare example of women associated with treasure hunting. Kieckhefer, *Magic in the Middle Ages*, 151; Ryrie, *Sorcerer's Tale*, 101–7; Anon., *The Brideling, Sadling and Ryding, of a Rich Churle in Hampshire, by the Subtill Practise of One Iudeth Philips, a Professed Cunning Woman, or Fortune Teller Vvith a True Discourse of Her Vnwomanly Vsing of a Trype Wife, a Widow, Lately Dwelling on the Back Side of S. Nicholas Shambles in London, Whom She with Her Confer-ates, Likewise Cosoned: For Which Fact, Shee Was at the Sessions House without* New-Gate Arraigned, Where She Con-fessed the Same, and Had Iudgement for Her Offence, to Be Whipped through the Citie, the 14. Of February, 1594. Printed at London : By T[homas] C[Reede] and Are to Be Solde by William Barley, at His Shop in New-Gate Market, Neare Christ-Church, 1595 (London: T[homas] C[reede], 1595).

21. The importance of hunting is also in evidence in the William Neville case in chapter one: the potential appointment of his lower-status friend to the post of keeper of the hounds and his expedition to get a buck.

THE TEXTS

4.1. The Fashioning of the Scepter[22]

The scepter must be of the bay tree, near as big as your arm at the hand, and it must be just a cubit long, and the bark taken off it and so remain white, and without any painting. Then the master with his stole must take it in his hand and hold it straight, saying, "Oh, thou creature of God, thou scepter of regal dignity, I conjure thee by the immeasurable virtue of the most highest God, and by the wisdom of Solomon, which did use thee for a sign and token of the dignity of a king for the constraining of all evil spirits. By the fearful day of judgment, and by all evangelical powers, I adjure thee that thou shalt be unto this man N. a singular help in his conjurations, compellings, and occasions of all spirits whensoever he shall work in this art of science, and that thou may have the same virtue and strength that Solomon made thee for, and whensoever thou shalt be borne and held up, procure love unto the bearer. Grant this, O Jesus Christ, which God with the Father and the Holy Ghost reignest world without end. Amen."

This done, anoint thy scepter with balsam or *corpo balsamo* all over. Then give the Master the end of the scepter to kiss as he kneeleth, and take it in his hand and let him lay it where he will till he occupy it, as long as it be in a clean cloth [8v].

The lamina of the scepter:

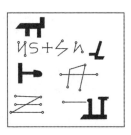

22. London, Wellcome Institute for the History of Medicine, Wellcome 110, fols. 8r–8v. Wellcome 110 is a sixteenth-century manuscript containing a variety of other conjuring works, including two versions of the *Thesaurus spirituum*. The first is an English epitome and reformulation of the text, from which we have extracted this passage; the second is the original Latin version.

Also, you shall understand that all these consecrations of the sword, ring, lamina, and scepter must be done upon a Friday in the hour of Venus, and that must be done the first Friday after the conjunction of the Sun and Moon. And look in any wise that the Friday be the second, fourth, sixth, [or] twenty-eighth day or else let it alone till the next Moon, for these be the days convenient.

4.2. For Treasure That Is Hid[23]

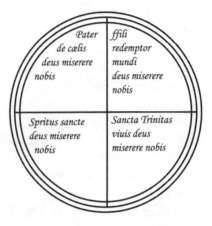

Jesus the Nazarene, King of the Jews, give us your grace. Amen.

In my name they will cast out demons, speak in new tongues, hold serpents. And if they drink poison, it will not kill them. In my name they will cast out demons; they will speak in new tongues; they will pick up snakes, and if they drink any deadly thing, it will not hurt them; they will lay their hands on the sick, and they will recover.[24]

23. Oxford, Bodleian Library, e Mus 173, fols. 66r–68r. This volume is a collection of conjuring material from the early seventeenth century. The passage is written in English. The use of the figure is unclear. The Latin text drawn from the *Litany of the Saints* reads clockwise from top left: "God, the Father of Heaven, have mercy on us. / God, the Son, the Redeemer of the world, have mercy on us. / Holy Trinity, one [read *unus*] God, have mercy on us. / God, the Holy Spirit, have mercy on us."

24. Mark 16:17–18. This passage and the short formula above it are in Latin.

Alleluja deus in nomine tuo, etc. *Deus misereatur,* etc.[25]

Thou spirit or spirits which keep this ground or earth and treasure, I conjure you and charge you by the mighty power of God and by his strength and by all the might, power, and strength of the holy and blessed Trinity, that thou or you depart, O thou spirit or spirits. I charge you and command you by all the power and strength of almighty God the Father of heaven, and by the virtue and divinity of Jesus Christ our Lord, coequal with the Father and with the Holy Ghost the third person of the Trinity, depart, o you spirit or spirits, I command you by the virtue, might, and strength of Jesus Christ the King of Glory, and by the virtue and love of the Holy Ghost and by all the strong mansions of Jesus Christ, king of all goodness, and by the virtue of the love and mercy of Jesus Christ, the only son of the living God, and by the virtue and obedience of Jesus Christ when he was obedient to the death of the cross, which liveth and reigneth with God his Father and the Holy Ghost in the perfect Trinity.

I conjure thee, thou spirit or spirits, by the fearful power of the judgment of him which shall judge all mankind and all kings and devils and all wicked spirits.

I conjure thee, thou spirit or you spirits by him to whom all knees do bow both in Heaven and Earth and Hell. Depart, o you spirit or spirits, from this place or ground and treasure and that thou or ye come not nigh unto it by the space of a hundred miles until we have taken and obtained our wills and pleasures by the virtue of the Holy Ghost and predestination of God in whose name I command thee thou spirit or you spirits that keep this treasure to depart from this place or ground and not to come nigh unto it by the space of a hundred miles neither to vex, trouble, nor fear us until we have had our full mind and pleasure.

I conjure thee, you spirit or you spirits, by the virtue of all heavens and celestial creatures worshipping the omnipotent God. Depart, o thou spirit or spirits, from this place and ground through the virtue of almighty God and of all earthly things, both quick and dead, moveable [66v] and unmovable, worshipping the omnipotent God. Depart, o

25. Incipits for Pss 53 and 66
(Vulg.).

thou spirit or spirits, from this place through the virtue of the person of Jesus Christ and of the sweet face of Jesus Christ, which was smitten upon and which spittle deformed, so be you spirit or spirits smitten with the fire and pains of hell, which shall always burn and never be quenched, if you depart not by and by from this place and ground and come not near it by a hundred miles until we have obtained our minds. Through the virtue and strength of rope, which bound the arms of Christ, wherewith he was drawn and stretched upon the cross, so be ye spirit or spirits drawn, stretched, and nailed with the most strongest pains of Hell with fiery chains except [if] ye depart by and by. Depart, o thou spirit or spirits, by the great pain the which Christ suffered in his feet when he was nailed upon the cross, so be you or ye spirit or spirits nailed and pierced with the pains of hellfire, except if you depart by and by. And if ye depart not by and by, the fire of hell, which shall always burn and never be quenched, descend and fall down upon you spirits and burn you so that you shall never have rest nor ease. And as the spear painfully pierced the side of Jesus Christ, so be ye spirit or spirits painfully pained so that you from this day forth shall never have rest nor ease. All thunders and lightnings with all the fire of Hell fall down upon you. The sword of death with all the torments of all the devils in Hell descend down upon you and remain upon you forever, except if ye depart incontinent from this place and ground and not to come near it by a hundred miles until we have taken out minds and pleasures therein. Depart, o you spirit or spirits. I conjure you and charge you by the virtue of the blood of the savior of all mankind and by the virtue of the blood and water that Christ sweated[26] upon the Mount of Olives before his bitter passion when he was in agony and the angel of God comforted him, declaring to him what a great mystery he should bring to pass through his blessed death, of the which mystery, o ye wicked spirit or spirits that keep this treasure, be no partakers but such as believe in his death. Depart from this place, o ye wicked spirit or spirits, I charge and command you by the infinite word of God that ye come not near it by the space of a hundred miles for the space of a hundred days next following, neither to trouble, vex, nor delude us, neither to draw it deeper nor lower into the earth, but

26. = bled

only to let it remain [67r] where it standeth without craft, falsehood, guile, or dissimulation, neither to change it into any other color but to let it remain as it is in its²⁷ own proper place.

I conjure ye, spirit or spirits, by the words that Christ spake in the time of his most blessed passion when he prayed for them that prosecuted him, saying, "Father, repute not this unto them for they know not what they do" and by these words which he spake to his holy mother, saying, "Woman, behold thy son," and to his disciples, "Behold thy mother," and by that holy word, "I thirst" (that is, the health of mankind), and by these words "Eloy, Eloy, Lamazabathianie," that is to say, "My God, my God, why has thou forsaken me?" and by these words, "It is ended," and by these holy words, "Father into thy hands I commend my spirit." Depart, ye spirit or spirits, from this treasure and from this place or ground by and by without any craft or guile or any manner of deceit.

I conjure you, spirit or spirits, by the virtue of Christ's passion and his resurrection, and also by the virtue of his holy ascension, and by the fearful coming of him to judgment, where ye and all your fellows shall receive just judgment, meet and according to your offenses, except ye depart from this place and ground. The virtue of the omnipotent God, the Father of all saints in Heaven, excommunicate you, and all his angels excommunicate and cast you into the everlasting pains and fire of hell where [there] never shall be comfort nor hope, ease nor rest. And Christ the only begotten son of the Father curse you and bind you with all the pains aforesaid. The Holy Ghost with all the church of God excommunicate you and curse you from all hope and forgiveness. The Holy Trinity curse and excommunicate you. All the sorrows, pains, and torments of Hell fall down upon you and remain upon you until the last day of doom, except ye depart immediately. All fires and lightnings and thunders curse you. All sorrow and malediction fall down upon you and remain upon you forever, o ye rebelling spirits, except ye now depart and neither hurt, trouble, nor vex us, nor draw nor convey away treasure from us, but suffer it to remain in this place here that we may obtain it, without craft, subtlety, or guile

27. *ye*

of you or any of you, by virtue of all that is afore spoken or shall be hereafter spoken. Amen.

I conjure you spirits and constrain you and command you that ye depart from this place and treasure and that ye come not near it by a hundred miles for the space of a hundred days next following.

I conjure you spirits by the first word that God spake in the creation of the world, saying, "Let there be light." And so it was done.

The second word he said, "Let there be a firmament between the waters and let it divide the waters." And so it was done.

The third word that God said, "Let the matter under heaven gather themselves [67v] together into one place that the dry land may appear." And so it was done.

The fourth word was when he commanded the trees and herbs to spring, saying, "Let the earth bring forth green grass that beareth seed and fruitful trees, every one in his kind bearing fruit." And so it came to pass.

The fifth word was when God made the Sun and the Moon and the stars, saying, "Let there be lights in the firmament of heaven to divide the day from the night that there may be tokens, signs, days and years, and let them be lights in the firmament to shine upon the earth." And so it was done.

The sixth word was when he made the fishes and fowls, saying, "Let the waters bring forth fishes that move and have life and fowls that fly under the firmament of heaven." And so it came to pass.

The seventh word was when God blessed them, saying, "Grow and multiply upon the earth."

The eighth word was when God said, "Let the earth bring living beasts, every one in his kind, and creeping worms." And so it was done.

The ninth was when God made man, saying, "Let us make man in our similitude after our likeness that he may have rule over fishes of the sea and fowls under heaven and over all cattle and over all the earth and over all worms that creep upon the earth."

The tenth word was when God said, "Grow and multiply you and fulfill the earth, subdue it, and have dominion over the fishes of the sea and over the fowls of the air and over all beasts and worms that creep upon the earth."

By virtue of all these words and of all the names of God, I conjure and compel you, o ye spirit or spirits, and straightly command you to depart from this place and treasure and neither convey it nor draw it lower nor change it into any other color or colors, but only to let it remain in its[28] own proper substance as it was when it was first set here and not to come near it by a hundred miles until such time as we have fulfilled our minds and wills and purposes. In the name of God the Father, of God the Son, and of God the Holy Ghost. Amen.

He that doth discharge the ground must be a priest having a stole about his neck and holy water and a bunch of hyssop to cast the holy water on the ground and turn his face into the East and read this above written [conjuration] three times devoutly.

This was written in a sheet of parchment, having on the back side thereof at every corner, a cross and one in the midst.

4.3. Getting Demons to Bring You the Treasure[29]

Now I have taught thee where, when, and whom thou shalt call. Now I shall teach thee how thou shalt call.

When thou are well disposed and sad in devotion as I have taught thee before, and that the time and weather is according and convenient to thy operation, and thy circle is hallowed, then with thy instruments necessary (that is to say sword, scepter, place, ring, and also coals and incense) with thy fellows, virtuously disposed, enter right sadly and devoutly as thou canst think into thy holy circle and deliver thy fellow the sword, which meekly kneeling to the ground he must receive. When you deliver it you must say:

"Brother, by virtue of the blood of Jesus Christ, I deliver this power that now you are able to touch, to hold, to govern with which and by which you will be able to restrain every fraudulence of malign spirits

28. *ye*
29. Oxford, Bodleian Library, e Mus
173 fols. 45v–47v. English.

through him who will come to judge the living and the dead and the world by fire."[30]

Then he must sit down, turning his face into the east and thou must devoutly put the ring on thy little finger and take the scepter in thy right hand and turn thee outwards towards the habitation or place where the spirit is, saying devoutly and heartily this invocation following:

"O thou spirit, N., wherever you be, I call thee in the name of the eternal God. I conjure thee, N., by the might of the Father omnipotent and by the wisdom of the Son omnipotent and by the virtue of the Holy Ghost, the comforter, and by the holy and undivided trinity of God and by all the holy names of God and especially by the might and virtue of these holy names following: + Tetragramaton + Iesum + Alpha + et Omega + Agyos + Emanuel + Agla + Usyon + Basyen + Christe + Sabaoth + Adonay + Panton + Craton + Iesus + Messias + Medikym + Medycyny + Helvecie + Hekesy + Heben + Medon + Thrabanna + Zno + Haday + Filioboy + Oba + Abba + Semapheras + and by all the other names of God by which you may be constrained commanded or bound [46r].

"I conjure, constrain, and command thee by the miracles and all the marvelous deeds of our Lord Jesus Christ, and by all his pains and passions that he suffered in his glorious body, and by his marvelous nativity and by his annunciation, and by his circumcision, and by his tribulation, scourging, and beating, and by his precious death, which

---

30. This passage is in corrupt Latin and the translation is speculative: "*Frater, per vertutem sanguinis Iesu Christi doliberam* [read *delibero*] *potestatem vt nunc gladium benedictum tangere tenere gubernare valeas cum quo.* *et per quem. omnis fraudolosa* [read *fraudulentia*] *malignorum spiritum* [read *spirituum*] *potestas* [read *potest*] *compescare. per eum qui venturus est iudicare vivos et mortuos et fielum* [read *saeculum*] *per ignem.*"

he meekly and graciously suffered to redeem mankind, and by his descent into Hell where he bound Lucifer and brought his well-beloved children out of the lamentation and pains of Hell to the joys of Paradise, and by his might, resurrection, and by his marvelous ascension, and by the might and virtue of him when he shall come in the end of the world and judge me and thee and all the creatures to their deserving through his righteousness.

"I conjure thee, N., by our blessed lady Saint Mary, the virgin undefiled, mother to our savior, Jesus Christ, queen and virgin and lady of the world, queen of heaven and empress of Hell, and by the virginity and chastity of that most glorious virgin, and by the marvelous fecundity, meekness, and obedience of her, and by all her holiness and innocence, and by all her joy both in earth and Heaven, and by all the dolors, pains, and tribulations that she suffered meekly here in this present world, and by all the prayers that ever she said, and by all the alms that ever she did, and by all her miracles that ever she wrought, and by all her goodness and mightiness.

"I conjure thee, N., by the Father, the Son, and the Holy Ghost, and by all the relics of saints which are in any place of the world, by the precious body and blood of our Lord Jesus Christ, and by the holy cross that our Lord Jesus Christ was nailed upon, and by the nails that were stricken through his hands and feet, and by the crown of thorns that was set upon his head, and by all the bodies and bones of saints contained within the world, and by all virtues of the Old Testament, by our mother the holy church, and by all masses, prayers, and alms deeds through the world to the honor and love of almighty God, and by all the ministers on[31] earth, by all the seven sacraments of the holy church, and by the ten commandments of God, and by the seven works of mercy, and by the twelve articles of faith, and by the two tables of the old law given to Moses, and by the wand of Aaron that flowered, and by all the creatures of God.

"I conjure thee, N., by the Father, the Son, and the Holy Ghost, and by all the holy company of Heaven, by angels, archangels, and thrones, by dominations, powers,[32] cherubim, and seraphim and by every good angel, and by the orders of angels in which you were before thy fall,

---

31. *in*   32. *potestats*

and by all holy patriarchs, prophets, apostles, evangelists, disciples, martyrs, confessors, virgins, and saints, and by all the servants of God, and by their tribulation and penance, alms deeds, and holy works, by all [46v] their doctrine and clemency, and by the four evangelists of God and the virtue of them, and by all the characters and figures of Heaven by which you or any other spirit art bound or compelled, by the seven planets of the air and the twelve signs of the zodiac, by all the stars in the firmament and tokens therein, and by the four princes of spirits that are in the four parts of the world, they which have power of almighty God to grieve the earth, the sea, and the trees, by the seven kings of the seven planets, and by the four elements, and by all things which there sustain and bring forth, and by the virtue of all manner of herbs, stones, trees, and waters, and by all things that spring in the earth, and by all beasts, wild and tame, and by all things that creep in the earth, and by all manners of weather and times, and by Lucifer, the prince and king of wicked spirits, which is bound in Hell, and by the spirit that thou art obedient to, and to whom you art bound to obey whatsoever he be or whatsoever he be called, by all conjurations, extortions, tokens, or instruments whereby you may be constrained.

"I conjure and charge thee, N., by all the virtues of our Lord Jesus Christ, and by the angel that shall cry in a trumpet at the day of doom and shall say, "Venite, venite, venite!"[33] and by angels, thrones, dominations, virtues, principals, cherubim, and seraphim.

"I conjure and charge thee, N., by the pains of our Lord Jesus Christ, and by the precious death of the cross whereon he was hanged, and by the nails wherewith he was nailed, and by the spear that opened his side, and by the blood and water that flowed there out, and by the crown of thorns wherewith he was crowned, and by his death resurrection and ascension, and by the sevenfold graces of the Holy Ghost, and by the ring and seal of Solomon, and by the virtue of the sun that was dark and stones that cleaved and graves that opened and many dead bodies [that] have risen, and by the wand of Moses that divided the sea, and by the wand of Aaron that budded, and by the throne of God, and by the golden censors, and by the golden altar, and by the lamps set before God, and by the seats of all the holy saints.

33. = Come, come, come!

"I conjure and charge thee, you spirit N., by the glorious Virgin Mary the mother of God, Jesus Christ, and by the flesh and blood that God took of the Virgin Mary, and by these names of God, which he named with his own mouth, that is A. and Ya.[34] Saday. Emanuel. Sabath. Arfex. Damamestoras, and by this holy name, Adonay, that God shall say at midnight at whose voice all dead men both good and bad suddenly shall arise, and by this holy name, Sother, whereby all stones and buildings shall fall and men shall say to mountains, "Fall upon us," and by this holy name, Esyon, whereby God shall cast the devil and his members and all wicked folk into [47r] the pit of Hell and God shall lead with him all chosen folk into everlasting bliss.

"I conjure thee, N., only in the virtue or power of God, and by the virtue of him that hath made all this world of naught, and by the infinite might and power of him and his virtue, and by all his creatures visible and invisible, and by all heavenly things, words, and names, and by all earthly things, words, names, and by all infernal things, words, and names that any spirit may be compelled by, and by all extortions, exorcisms, conjurations, and precepts by which Solomon and other exorcists have bound and called and compelled any spirit,[35] and by all names that you shalt be compelled or constrained by at the dreadful day of judgment in which Almighty God omnipotent shall judge all creatures, and by the dreadful judgment that shall be given upon thee in the day when you and every creature shall know their everlasting state, and by him that shall be their judge and judge all the world, quick and dead. Defer you not wheresoever you be, but come in haste without any manner of letting or tarrying, without any manner of grievous storms or any grievous noise, and with out hurting or harming men or any of my fellows, or any other Christian man, or any other creature, but come to me visibly and appear in the shape of a fair man or an angel, not frightening[36] me in no manner of wise, and that you fulfill all my commandments that I, in the power of almighty God, shall charge thee, and also that you depart not without

34. Presumably this is a mistranscription of "α and ω"—i.e., Alpha and Omega.

35. This passage is a good illustration of the slippage between the terms "conjurer" and "exorcist." The two are more or less synonymous in ritual magic.

36. *fearing*

my license, till I give thee leave *per eum qui venturus est iudicare vivos et mortuos seculum per ignem.*[37] Amen."

Now I have taught thee the coming of them, that is to say, when, where, and how. Now I shall also show thee the last part of this treatise, that is how to have thy purpose, wherein there is no more to do, but when you hast them before thy presence, then make thy conclusion of thy conjuration, showing thy intent and answer them with sweet savors till they have followed thy purpose. Then command what you wilt, saying:

"I charge thee you spirit, N., that appearest here before this circle by virtue of this conjuration wherewith we have constrained thee, and by the virtue of the most holy and dreadful names of God, and by the virtue of this name + Te + tra + gra + ma + ton + that you go without any letting or frauds, making unto such a place, N., and bring with you the treasure that lies there. And if there be none that is lawful, I charge thee by the aforesaid conjuration and under pain of eternal damnation that [47v] thou bring unto me seven thousand pound of lawful money of England, either in silver or gold, from what ground you wilt, and set it within our circle, without any hurt or harming of me or any of my fellows. Also, I charge thee by the virtue of God's blessed passion, and by all his principal wounds, and by the operation of his holy blood, and by his resurrection, and by his ascension, that you go and come without any tarrying, and without any hurt or harming of me, or any earthly creature. + Fiat + fiat + fiat.[38] + Amen."

Now when you hast thine intents performed, then license them to depart in this manner following. First, say thy conjuration, then make this conclusion at this time, saying:

A discharge or license: "Depart and go to your places where God hath ordained you to abide, without any grievous noise or storms, and at all times when I call you again to come quickly without any manner of tarrying and fulfill my intents. Depart now.[39] Depart now. Depart now, by the virtue of the holy Trinity and by every virtue of Heaven,

37. = by him who will come to judge the living and the dead and the world with fire

38. = Let it be done, let it be done, let it be done!

39. This last portion is in Latin.

and by the virtue of these names of God + A + g + l + a + Aglaya + Aglaoth + Te + tra + gra + ma + ton + and by virtue of every secret name of God, and by the virtue of our Lord Jesus Christ, who will come to judge the living and the dead and the world with fire. Let that father of love, the peace of our Lord Jesus Christ be between us and you. Let it be done. Let it be done. Let it be done. Amen. In the name of the Father and of the Son and of the Holy Ghost. Amen."

Then say, "In the beginning was the word, etc." up to the end of the gospel.[40]

4.4. Parchment Conjuring Circle 1[41]

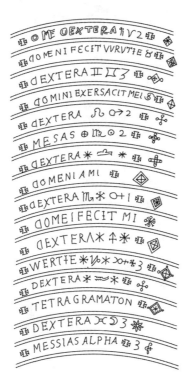

40. I.e., recite the first chapter of the Gospel of John.

41. Oxford, Bodleian Library, e Mus 173, fols. 68v–69r. This volume is a collection of conjuring material from the early seventeenth century. These sixteen arcs were meant to be assembled as a circle.

The length of this circle must be 12 yards, three quarters, and the breadth of it must be an inch at the least. And it must be cut compass that it may be round that length. Finis.

4.5. Parchment Conjuring Circle 2[42]

within this Circle must the master sit

here his fellowes

42. London, British Library, Additional 36674, fol. 157r. This volume contains a diverse variety of magic texts of the sixteenth and seventeenth century in diverse hands. This image is part of a fragmentary conjuring text written toward the end of the sixteenth century, seemingly unrelated to the surrounding text.

4.6. The Lamina of Oberion[43]

Say in the beginning of this experiment:

"*Veni creator*, etc. *Deus in nomine tuo*, etc. *Ad te levavi occulos*, etc. *Miserere mei deus*, etc. *Deus misereatur*, etc. *De profundis*, etc. *Kirieleison Christe eleison Kirie eleson. Pater noster*, etc."[44]

Prayer for power:

"I call upon you Agios, father of lights, Adonay, builder of all human flesh, Ely, of immense majesty, that you not abandon me in the time of my need, when my strength deserts me.[45] O Ruler of Rulers, King of Kings, king of the whole world, prophet most high, God of Abraham, God of Isaac, God of Jacob, God omnipotent, keep me from all evil and keep me from all evils and dangers, and from our enemies, and from the coming of spirits that they have power neither of touching nor of harming nor of terrifying me, for the love of your most sweet mother Mary and of all your saints who have been pleasing to you from the origin of the world right up to this hour. Amen."

Begin to operate on the day of the Moon in a waxing Moon. Make a lead or silver lamina and carve in it the image of the said spirit and its name on the front, with silver, and the name of the angel of the sun, which is Storax, and his sign over the name, and after that the name of the angel of the moon, that is Carmelion, and his sign over it. [62v]

Then say:

"O you Angels of the Sun and Moon, I ask and conjure you by the power of the highest God, On and Hel,[46] and by that wondrous name, that is, Hel, and by he who formed you, and through the signs,

43. London, British Library, Sloane 3318, fols. 62r–65r. This volume is a substantial early seventeenth-century conjuring manual. The passage is in Latin.

44. Incipits of various elements of the liturgy that were supposed to be performed in full and in Latin. *Veni creator spiritus* is a well-known medieval hymn. Following this are the incipits for Pss 54 (53), 123 (122), 51 (50), 67 (66), and 130 (129), indicating that each of these psalms was to be recited in full. This is to be followed by the *Kyrie eleison*, a common liturgical element. The whole concludes with the Lord's Prayer.

45. Ps 71:9

46. = El

which are sculpted in this lamina, and by the virtue of our omnipotent creator and in the name of the sublime God that whenever I will have invoked Oberion, whose name and image are sculpted in this lamina, that you should make that Oberion obey me and appear in this mirror in a beautiful human form, not harming to me nor to anyone else on earth. I conjure you angels of the Sun and Moon by the names of the most high omnipotent god living and true, Hee, Hot, Isacas, Clastia, Esma, Ebel, Agla, Antasa, Carihuata, Ziro, Rusa, Gallus, Merile, Milerior, Ergeth, Foras, Gramaton, Aglanatus, Sagite, Elimaron, Elomes, Fetida, Ebo, Leromisaza, Aquamebel, Sagesius, Zonas, and Senamon, that whenever I will have invoked Oberion, whose name and image are sculpted in this lamina, you make that Oberion obey me and appear to me in this mirror in a beautiful human form, and that he serve me according to my desire without contrivance, deceit, or falsehood, and perfectly and truly to fulfill my desire in everything."

And do no more the first day [63r].

In the second day write in the aforesaid lamina the name of his counselor, which is Caberion, with his sign in the right part of the image, and say:

"I conjure you spirit Caberion, by every celestial, terrestrial, and infernal thing, and by King Solomon, who subjugated you to himself, and by all of his signs, sigils, and rings, and by the elements though which the whole world is nourished, and by the serpent lifted up in the wasteland,[47] that you give counsel to your lord Oberion that he show himself to me and, according to his ability, truly bring about my desire whenever I invoke him."

And say this twice, three times in the day, and once in the night.

In the third day, write in the said lamina on the left hand of the image the name of his second counselor, who is Severion, and his sign. And say:

"O you Severion, I conjure you and command you by these names, Eloy, Elliar, or Elirom, that no one ought to name unless in danger of

47. John 3:14

death or dire straights, and by every spirit, as with inferior so with superior, that without any delay you give your lord counsel that he show himself companionable to me in all things and accomplish my desire to all of his ability whenever I will have invoked him."

Then read the aforesaid names by saying:

"I conjure you Storax, Carmelion, Caberion [63v], and Severion, and I exorcize, invoke, and command that you go without any delay to Oberion, whose fellowship I desire and make that Oberion to obey me and appear to me in beautiful human form and to certify to me concerning everything of which I desire to interrogate him without deceit or artifice by the virtue of these names, Hel, Yra, Ytaky, Eythan, Colpuo, and Trapus, and by the true and living God who created the world from nothing and by all the angels and archangels, thrones, dominations, principalities, and powers and by every name of God with which you are able be bound."

Afterwards suffumigate the lamina and say this aforesaid conjuration in a secret location towards the east. And in the following night after the middle of the night between the hours 1 or 2 or 3, holding the lamen and image towards the east, say:

"O you Oberion, most dazzling spirit whose name and image are here inscribed, come, Oberion, I invoke you, show yourself a friend to me by the virtue of Ysus, Odos, Ioht, and by the virtue of the highest God, whom Arabic, Greek, and Chaldean law venerate, and all of his saints, and by the King in whose legion you are lingering and through the requests of those whose names are carved in this lamina and by their signs and by the virtue that you have, I conjure you that you come to me immediately in beautiful human form not harming me nor anyone [64r] else existing on Earth, but speedily come and accomplish my will."

And straightaway he will come and when he has responded to you concerning everything. The license for him thus:

"I conjure you, Oberion, that you immediately return to your proper place where God set you and be at hand whenever at another time I shall invoke you, in the name of the Father, and of the Son, and of the Holy Spirit, Amen. And peace be between us and you."

And make a suffumigation of frankincense.

The Characters serving for this design are previously described, and in the second book of Lombard, or you may use these following.

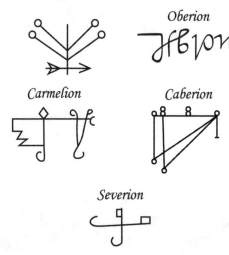

Storax or better Stopax

Oberion

Carmelion

Caberion

Severion

Conclusion

The sources considered here demonstrate the working assumption of most historians, that English authorities tended to confront real magic practitioners only in grievous cases or when the magic threatened social, religious, or political order. The punishments were also far less extreme than called for either in legislation or in the stated intentions of church and state. Even in the relatively unusual case of the Mixindale Fellowship, the rumor and disrepute brought upon the church by the three priests was as critical to the case as the heretical nature of their magic. Similarly, the punishments were limited to public penance or periods of imprisonment. Finally, the authorities could have pursued these cases further. They could have followed the leads provided by the witnesses and the accused to find other magicians, the providers of their books and equipment, or the magicians' other clients. Instead, the investigations appear to have been limited to those immediately involved.

The myth of the solitary learned magician, sometimes implied by texts of magic like the *Ars notoria* and often tacitly assumed in the analysis of magic manuscripts, is not borne out by these cases. The magicians were not isolated and solitary but operated in informal networks in which communities of lay and clerical practitioners, as well as learned and less learned ones, cooperated with each other and exchanged materials, books, and even clients. Moreover, those styled as "cunning men" trafficked in what is commonly understood as learned magic, and learned magicians were referred to as "cunning," demonstrating that the lines between cunning folk and the scribes of learned magic are far from clear. Future analysis of magic manuscripts should certainly assume that the scribes might have been not only active practitioners but also regarded by their communities as cunning folk.

Legal documents also reveal other critical elements in our under-standing of the practice of learned magic. They reveal magicians strug-gling to make sense of the rituals, their doubts about them, or their creative modifications, such as in the Mixindale Fellowship's debates over the singing breads or Steward's idea that the conjurer should stand outside the magic circle. They also reveal the social world of the magicians, their search for clients, and the forms of patronage they accepted. Just as critically, they reveal overlapping areas of practice that may be invisible in the manuscripts, such as alchemy and the peddling of prophecies. These in turn demand that we reconsider what it meant to be a magician or cunning man in the early Tudor period.

BIBLIOGRAPHY

MANUSCRIPT SOURCES

Cambridge, University Library
    Additional 3544
London, British Library
    Additional 36674
    Harley 2267
    Royal 17.A.XLII
    Sloane 3318
    Sloane 3822
    Sloane 3826
    Sloane 3846
    Sloane 3847
    Sloane 3850
    Sloane 3853
London, Wellcome Institute for the History of Medicine
    Wellcome 110
    Wellcome 1466
Oxford, Bodleian Library
    Bodley 951
    e Mus 173
    e Mus 238
    Rawlinson D. 252
Washington, Folger Shakespeare Library
    Vb 28

ARCHIVAL SOURCES

London, The National Archives of the United Kingdom (TNA)
    TNA E 163 10/20
    TNA SP 1/69/12
    TNA SP 1/69/15

TNA SP 1/72/172r–174r; 175r–178v; 179r; 180r
TNA SP 1/73/1r
TNA SP 1/75/38r; 39r
TNA SP 1/238
York, Borthwick Institute for Archives
Abp. Reg. 26 Christopher Bainbridge (1509–1514), fols. 68r–72v.

PUBLISHED PRIMARY SOURCES

Anon. *The Brideling, Sadling and Ryding, of a Rich Churle in Hampshire, by the Subtill Practise of One Iudeth Philips, a Professed Cunning Woman, or Fortune Teller Vvith a True Discourse of Her Vnwomanly Vsing of a Trype Wife, a Widow, Lately Dwelling on the Back Side of S. Nicholas Shambles in London, Whom She with Her Conferates, Likewise Cosoned: For Which Fact, Shee Was at the Sessions House without New-Gate Arraigned, Where She Confessed the Same, and Had Iudgement for Her Offence, to Be Whipped through the Citie, the 14. Of February, 1594. Printed at London : By T[homas] C[Reede] and Are to Be Solde by William Barley, at His Shop in New-Gate Market, Neare Christ-Church, 1595.* London: T[homas] C[reede], 1595.
Caesarius of Heisterbach. "Dialogus miraculorum." In *The Dialogue on Miracles*, edited by Henry von Essen Scott and C. C. Swinton Bland. London: Routledge, 1929.
Hedegård, Gösta, ed. *Liber iuratus Honorii—A Critical Edition of the Latin Version of the Sworn Book of Honorius.* Stockholm: Almovist & Wiksell International, 2002.
"Henry VIII: Miscellaneous, 1534." In *Letters and Papers, Foreign and Domestic, Henry VIII*, vol. 7, 1534, ed. J. S. Brewer and James Gairdner, 599–627. London, 1883. British History Online http://www.british-history.ac.uk/letters-papers-hen8/vol7/pp599-627.
Humphreys, K. W. *The Friars' Libraries.* Corpus of British Medieval Library Catalogues. London: British Library in association with the British Academy, 1990.
John of Salisbury. "Policraticus." In *Frivolities of Courtiers and Footprints of Philosophers: Being a Translation of the First, Second, and Third Books and Selections from the Seventh and Eighth Books of the Policraticus of John of Salisbury.* Translated by Joseph B. Pike. Minneapolis: University of Minnesota Press, 1938.
Letters and Papers, Foreign and Domestic, Henry VIII. Edited by J. S. Brewer and James Gairdner. 21 vols. London, 1875. British History Online. http://www.british-history.ac.uk/letters-papers-hen8.
Neville, William. *The Castell of Pleasure . . . : The Text of the First Issue of the Poem, with Variant Readings from the Reprint of 1518.* Edited by Roberta D. Cornelius. Oxford: Oxford University Press for the Early English Text Society, 1930.

Reformatio Legum Ecclesiasticarum, Ex Authoritate Primum Regis Henrici. 8. Inchoata: Deinde Per Regem Edouardum 6. Prouecta, Adauctaque in Hunc Modum, Atque Nunc Ad Pleniorem Ipsarum Reformationem in Lucem Ædita. London: 1641.

Scot, Reginald. *The Discoverie of Witchcraft.* London: W. Brome, 1584.

Thabit ibn Qurra. "De Imaginibus." In *The astronomical works of Thabit b. Qurra,* edited by Francis J. Carmody, 167–97. Berkeley: University of California Press, 1960.

Thetel. "De Imaginibus." In "*Cethel aut veterum Judaeorum Phisilogorum de Lapidibus Sententie,*" in *Spicilegium Solesmense III,* edited by J. B. Pitra, 335–37. Paris: Institutus Franciae, 1852.

PUBLISHED SECONDARY SOURCES

Bailey, Michael D. "The Feminization of Magic and the Emerging Idea of the Female Witch in the Late Middle Ages." *Essays in Medieval Studies* 19 (2002): 120–34.

Briggs, K. M. *The Anatomy of Puck: An Examination of Fairy Beliefs Among Shakespeare's Contemporaries and Successors.* London: Routledge & Kegan Paul, 1959.

Bruschi, Caterina, and Peter Biller. *Texts and the Repression of Medieval Heresy.* York Studies in Medieval Theology. Woodbridge, UK: York Medieval Press; Rochester, NY: Boydell & Brewer, 2003.

Camille, Michael. "Visual Art in Two Manuscripts of the Ars Notoria." In *Conjuring Spirits: Texts and Traditions of Medieval Ritual Magic,* edited by Claire Fanger, 110–39. Stroud: Sutton, 1998.

Cohen, Thomas. "Three Forms of Jeopardy: Honor, Pain, and Truth-Telling in a Sixteenth-Century Italian Courtroom." *Sixteenth Century Journal* 29, no. 4 (1998): 975–98.

Collins, Arthur. *Collin's Peerage of England.* 9 vols. N.p., 1812.

Coote, Lesley A. *Prophecy and Public Affairs in Later Medieval England.* York: York Medieval Press, 2000.

Davies, Owen. *Cunning-Folk: Popular Magic in English History.* London: Hambledon and London, 2003.

Davis, Natalie Zemon. *Fiction in the Archives: Pardon Tales and Their Tellers in Sixteenth-Century France.* The Harry Camp Lectures at Stanford University. Stanford: Stanford University Press, 1987.

Devine, Michael. "John Prestall: A Complex Relationship with the Elizabethan Regime." MA thesis, Victoria University of Wellington, 2010.

Dillinger, Johannes. *Magical Treasure Hunting in Europe and North America: A History.* New York: Palgrave Macmillan, 2012.

Elton, G. R. *Policy and Police: The Enforcement of the Reformation in the Age of Thomas Cromwell.* Cambridge: Cambridge University Press, 1972.

Harkness, Deborah E. *John Dee's Conversations with Angels: Cabala, Alchemy, and the End of Nature.* Cambridge: Cambridge University Press, 1999.

Jaech, Sharon L. Jansen. "The 'Prophisies of Rymour, Beid, and Marlyng':
    Henry VIII and a Sixteenth-Century Political Prophecy." *Sixteenth
    Century Journal* 16, no. 3 (1985): 291–300.

Jansen, Sharon L. *Political Protest and Prophecy Under Henry VIII*. Wood-
    bridge, UK: Boydell Press, 1991.

Kieckhefer, Richard. "Erotic Magic in Medieval Europe." In *Sex in the Middle
    Ages: A Book of Essays*, edited by Joyce E. Salisbury, 30–55. New York:
    Garland, 1991.

———. *Forbidden Rites: A Necromancer's Manual of the Fifteenth Century*. [In
    English and Latin.] Stroud: Sutton, 1997.

———. *Magic in the Middle Ages*. Cambridge: Cambridge University Press,
    2000.

Klaassen, Frank. "Curious Companions: Spirit Conjuring and Alchemy in the
    Sixteenth Century." In *Knowing Demons, Knowing Spirits in the Early
    Modern Period*, edited by Michelle D. Brock, Richard Raiswell, and
    David Winter, 145–70. London: Palgrave Macmillan, 2018.

———. "Learning and Masculinity in Manuscripts of Ritual Magic of the Later
    Middle Ages and Renaissance." *Sixteenth Century Journal* 38, no. 1
    (2007): 49–76.

———. *Making Magic in Elizabethan England*. University Park: Pennsylvania
    State University Press, 2019.

———. "Ritual Invocation and Early Modern Science: The Skrying Exper-
    iments of Humphrey Gilbert." In *Invoking Angels*, edited by Claire
    Fanger, 341–66. University Park: Pennsylvania State University Press,
    2011.

———. *The Transformations of Magic: Illicit Learned Magic in the Later
    Middle Ages and Renaissance*. University Park: Pennsylvania State
    University Press, 2013.

Klaassen, Frank, and Katrina Bens. "Achieving Invisibility and Having
    Sex with Spirits: Six Operations from an English Magic Collection
    ca. 1600." *Opuscula: Short Texts of the Middle Ages and Renaissance* 3,
    no. 1 (2013): 1–14.

Lambert, Malcolm. *Medieval Heresy: Popular Movements from the Gregorian
    Reform to the Reformation*. 3rd ed. Oxford, UK: Blackwell 2002.

Maxwell-Stuart, P. G. *The British Witch: The Biography*. Stroud: Amberley,
    2014.

Midelfort, H. C. Erik. "Witch Craze? Beyond the Legends of Panic." *Magic,
    Ritual, and Witchcraft* 6 (2011): 11–33.

Mowat, Barbara A. "Prospero's Book." *Shakespeare Quarterly* 52, no. 1 (2001):
    1–33.

Murray, James A. H. *The Romance and Prophecies of Thomas of Erceldonne
    Printed from Five Manuscripts; with Illustrations from the Prophetic
    Literature of the 15th and 16th Centuries*. Early English Text Society.
    London: Trubner, 1875.

Neal, Derek. "Suits Make the Man: Masculinity in Two English Law Courts, c. 1500." *Canadian Journal of History* 37, no. 1 (April 2002): 1–22.

Parish, H. L. "London, John (1485/6–1543), Administrator." *Oxford Dictionary of National Biography.* September 23, 2004. https://doi.org/10.1093/ref: odnb/16957.

Raine, James. "Proceedings Connected with a Remarkable Charge of Sorcery, Brought Against James Richardson and Others, in the Diocese of York, A.D. 1510." *Archaeological Journal* 16 (1859): 71–81.

Rider, Catherine. *Magic and Impotence in the Middle Ages.* Oxford: Oxford University Press, 2006.

———. *Magic and Religion in Medieval England.* London: Reaktion, 2012.

———. "Medical Magic and the Church in Thirteenth-Century England." *Social History of Medicine* 24, no. 1 (2011): 92–107.

Ryrie, Alec. *A Sorcerer's Tale: Faith and Fraud in Tudor England.* Oxford: Oxford University Press, 2008.

Turner, Dawson. "Brief Remarks Accompanied with Documents Illustrative of Trial by Jury, Treasure-Trove, and the Invocation of Spirits for the Discovery of Hidden Treasure in the Sixteenth Century." *Norfolk Archaeology or Miscellaneous Tracts Relating to the Antiquities of the County of Norfolk* 1 (1847): 41–64.

Véronèse, Julien. "Magic, Theurgy, and Spirituality in the Medieval Ritual of the *Ars Notoria.*" In *Invoking Angels*, edited by Claire Fanger, 37–78. University Park: Pennsylvania State University Press, 2012.

Victoria County History. *A History of the County of York.* Edited by William Page. Vol. 3. London: Victoria County History, 1974.

Weill-Parot, Nicolas. *Les "images astrologiques" au Moyen Âge et à la Renaissance.* Paris: Honoré Champion, 2002.

Wordsworth, Christopher. *Ceremonies and Processions of the Cathedral Church of Salisbury.* Cambridge: Cambridge University Press, 1901.

Wright, Sharon Hubbs, and Frank Klaassen. *Everyday Magicians in Tudor England: Legal Records and Magic Manuscripts.* Forthcoming.

Young, Francis. *The Cambridge Book of Magic: A Tudor Necromancer's Manual.* [Text in Latin containing passages in Middle English, with parallel translation in English; introduction and notes in English.] Ely, UK: Francis Young, 2015.

———. *Magic as a Political Crime in Early Modern England.* London: Taurus, 2018.

Zambelli, Paola. *The Speculum Astronomiae and Its Enigma: Astrology, Theology, and Science in Albertus Magnus and His Contemporaries.* Boston Studies in the Philosophy of Science 135. Dordrecht; Boston: Kluwer Academic, 1992.

INDEX

abstinence, 4
   See also purity, physical and
     spiritual
Act of Henry VIII 1542, 6–7, 9–10, 23
Agrippa von Nettesheim, Henry
     Cornelius, 4–5, 11, 43
alchemy, 12, 60, 62–63, 144
Allen, Robert, 10
Amaymon (spirit), 72, 74
Amylion (cunning man), 14–15
angels
   astral magic and, 3, 58
   in Jones's dream vision, 50
   lamina and conjuring of, 139–40
   in magic texts, 40, 60–61
   scrying and, 72, 74–75
   sigils and, 65
   in treasure hunting operations,
     133, 134
   See also demons
anger, mitigation of, 59
anxiety, 21, 23, 58, 123
apostasy, 88
Arabic magic, 1, 3, 58
Arden Wood (Yorkshire), 87, 98, 101,
     106, 117, 120
Ars notoria, 13, 58n3, 60–61, 143
astral magic, 2, 3, 58
astrology, 5, 11
Austin Friars library (York), 12, 117
authorities

cunning folk and, 5, 6
law, application of, 17
and magic, legality of, 1, 2, 6–11,
     16, 143
   See also ecclesiastical courts;
     secular courts
Avinell, Thomas, 22, 31, 32

Bacon, Friar, 47
Bainbridge, Christopher (Archbishop
     of York), 83, 88, 90, 110, 111, 113
balsam, 79, 125
Bank, Henry, 84, 87, 105–6, 119
baptism, 76, 109
Belphares (spirit), 87, 99, 101, 117
Bingley (Yorkshire), 83, 87–88,
     92–93, 100, 104
Boleyn, Anne, 31
Boxgrove Manual, 122n16
Bradford Fair, 88, 102
breads, singing. *See* loaves, singing
Buckingham, Duke of (Edward
     Stafford), 43

Caberion (spirit), 140, 141, 142
Cadwallader, 43
Caesarius of Heisterbach, 122
canon law, 17
   See also ecclesiastical courts
Carmelion (spirit), 139–40, 141, 142
Carver, John, 90, 110, 111, 113, 114, 115

Greenwood, Richard (*continued*)
in Mixindale case, 84, 85, 86, 87
penalties for, 113–14
in Richardson's confession, 92
in Stewart's confession, 107, 108
in Wilkinson's confessions, 101
in Wilson's confessions, 97–98
in Wood's confession, 104
Gres, Sir, 50
Greville, Giles, 23
Guy of Warwick, 45, 48

Hagh, Ottwell at
confessions of, 101–2
in Greenwood's confession, 105
in Knowles's confession, 103
in Mixindale case, 83, 84, 85, 86, 88
penalties for, 113–15
in Richardson's confession, 92
in Stewart's confession, 108
in Wilson's confessions, 97–98
Halywell (monk), 84, 96
Hancocks, John, 35
Hardwick, Christopher, 105
Hardwick, William, 106
Hardy, John, 100
Harington, James, 113
Harlock, William, 22, 30
See also Hurlock
hazel wands, 121n13
healing magic
charms and, 8
cunning folk and, 5
of magic practitioners, 13
sigils and, 65, 66–67, 68
Stewart and, 107
heavenly bodies, 3, 64
Henry VIII
in Jones's letters, 51
magic, legislation on, 6–7, 9–10, 23
in Neville's confession, 47
predictions on death of, 10, 25–26,
31–32, 34, 36, 37

heresy
ecclesiastical courts and, 8, 83, 88,
89, 90
Mixindale case and charges of, 90,
99, 103, 106, 111–12, 113, 143
Hermes, 50
holy water, 66, 86, 101, 103, 131
honor, magic for, 60, 66, 68–69
Howard, Thomas (Duke of Norfolk),
15–16, 55, 61–62
Hugh, Master, 22, 25, 33–34
hunting, 26, 37, 45, 124, 124n21
Hurlock, 22, 25, 30, 31, 45

ibn Bishr, Sahl, 58
illness. *See* healing magic
impotence, magic for, 67
influence, magic for, 60, 66, 68–69,
70
inheritance, 23
intelligence, magic for, 68
invisibility, magic of, 25, 32, 57, 63–64
invocations. *See* Jesus, invocation of;
spirit conjuring
isolation, 13

James 2:13, 51
Jameson, Thomas
articles against, 94–96
in brotherhood of magicians,
123–24
in Greenwood's confession, 104–5
in Hagh's confession, 102
imprisonment of, 111–12
in Knowles's confession, 102
magic texts and, 100, 117
in Mixindale case, 84, 85, 87–88
penalties for, 113–15
in Richardson's confession, 90–91,
92, 93–94
in Stewart's confession, 108, 109
in Wilkinson's confessions, 99,
100, 101
in Wilson's confessions, 97–99
Jansen, Sharon, 30